PRAISE FOR C
IN LOVE FROM ₁ᵗ EDITION
AMAZON REVIEWS

5.0 out of 5 stars Amazing book
Reviewed in the United States on August 19, 2023
Verified Purchase

"I was so excited to receive Mina's book, and I knew it was going to be life changing to me, like everything she shares. It was great reading through her story and the lessons she learnt. Even though I watched nearly all of her videos and have two of her courses, this book gave me a lot. I read it almost in one go and it nurtured my soul deeply. Thank you Mina." – Kamilla

5.0 out of 5 stars Sweet Kick in The Pants
Reviewed in the United States on July 26, 2023
Verified Purchase

"I purchased the Kindle version of this book in 2017 right after discovering Mina on YouTube. Even though this version of Mina no longer exists, there were sprinkles of the future Mina throughout this book. She is generous, loving, beautiful and highly intelligent. I am so grateful to have her wisdom and her teachings in my life. Thank you Mina." – Teency's Thoughts

5.0 out of 5 stars A guide for inner peace
Reviewed in the United States on August 3, 2023
Verified Purchase

"This book was easy to read and full of practical wisdom and advice that can be applied almost immediately. Thank you Mina." – Kirsy

5.0 out of 5 stars Very informative
Reviewed in the United States on February 24, 2023
Verified Purchase

"This book is very informative. In this book Mina gives advice on various topics. I have read this book once in one day. I couldn't stop reading. I am going to reread this book again soon. Thank you Mina for the wonderful advice you give us women and how you always look after us and teach us the feminine power and potential within us." – Maria

5.0 out of 5 stars I felt like I was getting advice from a wise older sister...
Reviewed in the United States on April 18, 2016
Verified Purchase

"This book is written in a conversational and loving tone. I felt like I was getting advice from a wise older sister who wants the best for me while also accepting my choices. Mina helps people look to themselves to take ownership of their lives. She is honest that you have to be willing to reflect on what you want, make that your mission and then set your point of attraction and make your decisions in alignment with your mission. She explains how she did this for her health, relationships, finances, and, most importantly, for self-love. I read this book on a plane ride home from a business trip and was so glad it was Friday because it inspired me to make several immediate changes when I got home. I really appreciate what Mina shares and feel that I have made positive shifts in my life because of her candor about her own life." – Christina

***5.0 out of 5 stars* Inspiration to change your life**
Reviewed in the United States on April 19, 2016
Verified Purchase

"Ever since becoming a mom 10 months ago I haven't had time to read. Thus, I turned to audiobooks for personal growth and entertainment. So this is the first book in almost a year that I have actually "read'. I can honestly say I loved it! I could hear Mina's voice in every single page of this book. It's as if she is whispering in your ear step by step instructions on how to become your best self. Even if you are not a follower of Mina's YouTube channel, you'll enjoy reading this personal book. Mina - I want to read more!" :) – The spicy Rose

***5.0 out of 5 stars* I have learned so much from Mina and I highly recommend her book to anyone**
Reviewed in the United States on May 13, 2016
Verified Purchase

"Mina has a very kind, straightforward way of speaking that both inspires and motivates you to make positive changes in your life. She focuses on wise introspection to create the life you want to have. She teaches unique mindsets that have immediate effects and is open and honest about her own struggles in life and how she overcame them. She is a strong believer of powerful transformation and lifelong learning. I have learned so much from Mina and I highly recommend her book to anyone!" – Jasmin Frick

***5.0 out of 5 stars* Simple and enlightening! A true gem of wisdom for any woman who wants to be a better person…**
Reviewed in the United States on January 20, 2021
Verified Purchase

"This was a quick and enlightening read! In this short book, Mina communicates the most important lessons she learned throughout her life and they are applicable to any woman who is willing to do the inner work and grow as a person. As a Christian who believes in Jesus, I do not necessarily believe the Law of Attraction and manifestation per se, but I was so fascinated by how much the core concepts of this book align with what the Bible teaches. Finding true inner peace with yourself and God (the Universe or another higher power you believe in), letting go of expectations and judgments of yourself and others and living with gratitude and joy every single day. Mina shows us even though there are hard things in life (losing loved ones, divorce, abuse, tragedy etc), we also have ownership in how we respond and move forward. In the end, we cannot control and change anyone else. We can only control our own selves and actions. The most important investment we can make in our lives is to constantly take time to look deep within ourselves, identify what truly matters to us, learn about our triggers and insecurities, own up to our past mistakes and learn from them, let go of choices, lifestyles and people that do not align with our core purpose. Truly learning to accept and love myself with all my human imperfections while simultaneously taking responsibility for my past faults, choosing forgiveness and compassion (for myself and others), and growing and evolving as a person. When we do this inner work, we have so much more grace and acceptance for ourselves and the people in our lives. Thank you Mina! I am learning so much from your YouTube channel. Even if I don't agree with some things, your core message resonates so much with me in my present moment. It must be kismet that I found you during this period in my life." - Yedidya

Contained in Love

Reclaiming Your Feminine Power as a Wife and Mother

Second Edition

MINA IRFAN

Contained in Love\ Mina Irfan – Second Edition

ISBN: 979-8-9890423-3-3 (Paperback)

ISBN: 979-8-9890423-4-0 (Ebook)

For Sheena and Alina

CONTENTS

Introduction. 14

1. What in the World do you Even Want? 18

2. Become Your Own Dream
Girl one Bite at a Time. 35

3. Fit Girl Era 50

4. One Confrontation away from Level 10 Cray .. 58

5. Get Off of Me. 66

6. Adulting. 74

7. Unbothered 81

8. Your Humans. 90

9. The Most Beautiful Woman in the Room. 99

10. Put your Money where your Soul is 115

11. Intersection of Identities. .. .. .125

References. .. .. .140

Additional Resources.. .. .. .142

Foreword

August 23, 2023

This may be the first forward ever to be written by the author's own future self. Let me explain. I am future Mina Irfan from August of 2023. When I wrote this book 7 years ago in 2016, I had no idea of the miraculous quantum leaps my life was about to take as a result of the inner work and process I wrote about in this book. I also had no clue that my transformation would start a revolution of inner work for hundreds of thousands of women worldwide. It's clear to me now that the old version of Mina was creating energetic space for a new, upgraded version to emerge.

In this new and expanded version of this book, I have left the original chapters mostly intact, only fixing a few typos here and there and adding in a phrase or two for more clarity. It was important for me to honor the journey of the original version of this book and message. Below each original chapter, I have added some notes from the perspective of the 2023 version of me. Those areas are clearly marked. I have also added an affirmation or two and some journal prompts at the end of each chapter for further reflection.

I hope you enjoy the journey of a deeply exhausted independent woman into finding her personal power and becoming nourished as a wife and mother. It gives me great pleasure to have documented my journey for you in 2016 and now having the honor of adding to it.

Oceans of Love,

Mina Irfan

August 23, 2023

Preface

Congratulations. You just picked up a relationship book about the most important relationship you will ever have in your lifetime. No, this book is not a quick, fix marriage how to. It's not even a parenting manual. Disappointed? Don't be. This book will help you re-set and transform your mindset and improve the most important relationship you have. The relationship with yourself. "But I already have a healthy relationship with myself, Mina." I can practically hear the whining start. If you have been following my YouTube channel, then you should know my response. There is always room for improvement. You don't stop growing or learning until the day you stop breathing. Taking the time to improve and be willing to work on yourself will have profound effects on your health, wealth, marriage, and all other aspects of your life. I guarantee it. It all starts from within. You are the only person with the permission and ability to change your life. We do not own other people and in turn others do not own us. Stop with the excuses and start with yourself. "But Mina you don't understand, my husband….." Just stop it. After over 5 years on YouTube speaking to and working with thousands of you, trust me I have heard it all. My answer is still the same. Only you have the power. You are in the driving seat of your life. You are in control.

I have always had a passion for writing, even as a little girl. It wasn't until I received a "Promising Young Authors of Illinois" award for writing something or another in my seventh-grade class that the thought of actually becoming an author came to my realm of possibilities. This book has resided in my heart and I can see now how the Universe has conspired my entire life to make this happen. You may be surprised to hear this book took 7 years in the making. I started writing it, which at the time was a "How to improve your marriage" nearly 7 years ago when my world was collapsing around me. Oh, to sit here and laugh while I imagine what a disaster of a book this would have turned out had I actually written it back then. I was trying to blend my 4-year-old son from a previous marriage into an exciting but totally awkward new marriage, battling an undiagnosed autoimmune disease, all while watching my mother being eaten alive by cancer. To say I was miserable would be a huge understatement. As I sat there depressed and working on the first few pages of my book, there was a constant nagging voice inside my head. "What the hell do you know about relationships?" I barely wrote the first few pages, filed it away and started a blog instead.

Little did I know at the time, the blog would eventually lead to a YouTube channel, friendships with women from all over the world, and a huge personal transformation. There was an amazing world on the other side of my despair. I was a caterpillar waiting to transform into a strong, amazing, gorgeous butterfly. To my surprise, I wasn't going to morph into this butterfly by fixing all the people and relationships around me. I could only achieve this dream by making myself a huge priority and working from within. And thus began the greatest transformation of my life.

A special thanks to my husband for giving me the emotional and physical space to write and for proofing and editing the final copy. And to my sons for their daily words of encouragement and love.

With Love & Gratitude,

Mina Irfan   2016

INTRODUCTION

In this book I want to share with you my journey to health, happiness, and lit from within joy. Ironically, the relationships I was so desperate to fix, the people so eager to impress, suddenly all magically fell into place once I truly started accepting, loving, and transforming myself. We're not talking about slapping on some lipstick and buying the right clothes or accessories and hoping for the best here. We are talking about a complete transformation of our mindset, health, wealth, and wisdom. You may be sitting there thinking, "My relationships are fine and I feel good, why is it even important?" Remember, there is always room for improvement. If you are the type of person that follows a positive thinking YouTube channel and picks up a self-help book, then you know this already and are here for a reason.

In starting this journey, I want you to forget everything you have been told by well-meaning relatives, fashion/dating magazines, and even your girlfriends. There really is no quick fix way of gaining control of your husband, in-laws, or even your kids. There are several key mindset switches that you will need to make. It's certainly a process and will take time, but just know that practice makes perfect. From today forward, you are your own religion. Practice, pray, and work on yourself like it's your business. Because guess what? It is your business. No one can do for you what YOU can do for you. You have to start this journey with the realization that we do not own other people. Once we can set others free from our control is when we can truly accept that others do not control us as well. You are a free person, with free will. No one, not even your husband or mother-in-law, can make you do anything without your permission. We make our own decisions and choices in life. If those decisions no longer serve us well, we always have the choice of choosing something better for ourselves.

You are your biggest asset. Seems too obvious and simple to me now, but I spent two long decades trying to please everyone else around me. I always figured my relationships, the money I made, and my friends were my biggest assets. What good are relationships, money, or even friends if you are not well or at peace with yourself? You will run through that money quickly in trying to buy your way through happiness. We all know how quickly store-bought happiness fades, and there is really no end in sight once you get on that roller coaster. Relationships and friends both have a strange habit of dissipating quickly when we are not happy and content people. Even relationships protected through DNA and marriage may crumble under the weight of constant negativity. Stop being the keeper of everyone else and literally stop, drop, and roll away. It's an emergency.

According to evolutionary psychologist Dr. Doug Lisle, our self-esteem is a direct result of the "rehearsals we do to please our internal audience."[1] Evolution strongly supports the need for social approval and acceptance into our tribes. Without this approval and acceptance, our ancestors had little chance of survival in the dangerous wild. The human race evolved to seek out this approval and acceptance from others. For those of us that say we don't care what other people think, what we are really saying is "we only care about what certain groups of people think and we ignore the rest." That group may be your family, social circles, or colleagues. Our internal audience is "our inner voice" that takes the essence of the groups of people we are trying to impress. So, in preparation for gaining that approval during our private "rehearsals," like when we eat right, work out, put on makeup, read, practice for a sport, or work on a project for our jobs, we are pleasing our internal audience. That audience gives us feedback depending on our efforts, preparing us for the approval and social acceptance we seek from those around us. Whether you actually care about pleasing other people or not, your self-esteem is based on the acceptance and approval you get from this internal audience.

When we take care of our bodies and put care and attention into our health, we receive positive feedback from this internal audience. "Wow, you're doing great. Your friends and family will surely notice all your efforts." This feeds our self-esteem and gives us confidence. So, if your goal is to lose weight, and you switch up your nutrition and start a fitness program, your internal audience immediately gives you positive feedback based on your efforts and boosts up your self-esteem even before your friends and family can see the changes in you. This encourages and motivates us to keep going, and work harder and harder. Once our family and friends do actually notice the changes, we receive positive feedback from them, which in return raises our esteem even further.

This makes complete sense from an evolutionary perspective, since being accepted in our tribes was essential to survival. If we did something socially unacceptable, the negative feedback we received from our tribe helped us change our behavior immediately. This internal audience was thus developed as a sort of feedback system to correct our mistakes and make improvements even before others noticed. Furthermore, we are designed to judge and choose a mate based on certain evolutionary advantages they have. According to Dr. Lisle, for females, beauty has been the most prized commodity in the entire animal kingdom (yes that includes us) since the dawn of time. Beauty, as you see, signals health, youth, and fertility. As much as you can argue that we have somehow risen above the animal kingdom and can overlook vanity, we are simply creatures of our esteem and the feedback from our peers that feeds that esteem. So how can you use this information to not only stand out in the crowd but also gain confidence and live a full, rich, and happy life? Let's dive deeper.

CHAPTER
One
WHAT IN THE WORLD DO YOU EVEN WANT?

To accomplish great things, we must not only act, but also dream; not only plan, but also believe. — *Anatole France*

If you were a business, what would your mission statement be? What are you all about? What are your goals, your aspirations, what do you want your legacy to be? It's amazing to me how many of us just stroll through life without any direction or mission. You are basically headed nowhere if you don't take the time to figure out what you want. Don't be the type of person that just goes through life doing all that is expected of them. Lurking from one mundane task to another without any clear, overall picture of where they are headed or what they want from life. It's time to take some ownership in the only true thing that belongs to you in this life. YOUR SELF. Here I would like to introduce the most powerful tool to gaining some focus and figuring out your life. Meet the pen and paper.

"But I have it all figured out in my head Mina." Oh, do you? With the overload of information, conflicting media messages, constant barrage of negative Facebook posts, visual distractions, and countless mindless mental drains, your anxiety prone self has it all figured out in your head? Stop it and think again. Sit down in a quiet, distraction free zone and start daydreaming on paper. What is the single most important goal in your life? What is the one thing you want to be remembered for in your life after you're gone? What is your legacy going to be? Get specific. Write down all descriptive words and phrases that come to mind.

My own personal journey started with the discovery of The Secret by Rhonda Byrne [2], after a heart wrenching divorce in 2006. Despite having a booming real estate business, being a full-time student at Northwestern University, and having an 18-month-old son to keep me busy and distracted, I was utterly devastated after my divorce. One day, I ended up seated at O'Hare airport, headed to see my cousin in Los Angeles. Just the day before, I had called her hysterically crying. After 18 months of a long dragged out, emotionally and physically draining process, my son and I were finally free from the man who completely shattered us into pieces. But I didn't feel free, I told her. Or happy. For months after the divorce, I had tried and kept myself busy and pulled together for my family's sake, but on the inside, I was completely falling apart. "You need to get away for a while," she suggested. "Get on the first flight here, I'm worried about you."

So, there I was, looking like a zombie, staring at a sea of people, trying to escape the pain that was weighing so heavily on my shoulders as I waited for my flight. "I know what you need," said a random voice sitting next to me. I looked to my right in despair. What a freak, I thought, is he seriously trying to hit on me at the airport? Can't he see what a mess I am right now! I guess he could. "You need to read The Secret," said the strange man sitting next to me. Okay, I'm done with this, I got up and walked into the airport book shop, trying to get away from this crazy person. As I stood there pretending to look at books, suddenly a familiar name popped out at me. The Secret by Rhonda Byrnes. Wow what a strange coincidence, I thought. I bought the book and stuffed it into my carryon, where it would sit forgotten for almost a year.

A year afterwards, as I was packing up once again, this time to move out of my parents' house and into my newly purchased condo, I rediscovered the book. I opened it up and read it, right then and there in one sitting, cover to cover, sitting among boxes of my belongings. Then read it again. Then again. Wow! I was amazed. Every single word in that book both touched my heart and slapped me in the face at the same time. All of a sudden it was becoming clear to me that I had a very active part in my divorce. I wasn't simply a victim; I was an active participant. "I caused my divorce,"

I wanted to scream out. You would think something so negative would make me feel bad or consume me with regret. Instead, I felt liberated! I felt free. For the first time I truly felt hope. I was so excited to learn about the Secret Movie DVD and soon started watching that on a daily basis.[3] I was amazed at what people had accomplished using the Law of Attraction and the power of visualizing their dreams. That led me to make a vision board of my own. And as they say, the rest is history. Thus began the first step towards my long transformation journey.

Through the process of realizing my goals and visualizing my dreams on this board, I started to learn a little more about myself. I wanted a better relationship with my son. I wanted to be the type of mother he deserved, not just the one everyone else expected me to be. One who was happy, healthy, and had it all together from the inside, not just the outside. I learned that while I enjoyed my real estate business and it paid the bills, I ultimately wanted to realize my dream of staying at home with my son, reading lots of books, and becoming a writer. Most of all, I wanted peace. The word "*Sukoon*" (meaning inner peace in Urdu) always took the biggest piece of real estate on my vision board. All these thoughts, which had been buried deep under the pressure of daily mundane tasks and the many responsibilities of a single mother, suddenly came pouring out on paper.

In early 2008 my life came crashing down on me once again. My mother, who was also my business partner, was suddenly diagnosed with stage 4 ovarian cancer. She was given 2 months to live by her doctors. Although I was devastated, my newfound religion, known as the Law of Attraction, kept me from feeling completely hopeless. I asked my mother to come stay with me after her surgery, and took the time to introduce her to The Secret. She instantly latched on to it and it gave her hope through what would become 2 years of a hellish fight against the biggest demon she ever faced.

My mother was a fighter and she was also an amazing salesperson. Although she knew I had vowed to never remarry after my previous heartbreak, she used the Law of Attraction to give me hope that there could be love again in my future. Around this time, one of my dear friends introduced me to his elder sister. She was a graceful woman, with a happy, loving marriage and 2 small children. I admired the relationship she had with her husband, children, her parents, siblings, and even her friends. I completely idolized her and admired the way she handled the many different roles in her life. She was so feminine and knew her place and role in society and I loved seeing her warmth and radiance! She gave me hope of having a happy, loving family.

Around this time, I caught an episode of Oprah, where a woman had attracted her dream man using a "love list." I decided it was time I used the Law of Attraction to make a "love list" for myself. I sat down in a quiet, distraction free zone and wrote the qualities I wanted in my perfect man. This was my chance to create the love of my life. He would be honest, loving,

WHAT IN THE WORLD DO YOU EVEN WANT?

and caring. A man of character, dignity, self-made, and trustworthy. He would love me, honor me, respect me, and cherish me.

A few months after I made this list, my mother and best friend started introducing me to potential suitors and I began rotational dating. Rotational dating is a process of dating for marriage that is common in my culture. Instead of becoming any one man's girlfriend, we get to know multiple suitors and their families to find the best match for us. I had several men on my rotation, and while they were all wonderful, none of them were the perfect match for my love list. My best friend suggested I make a profile on a matrimonial site that her siblings had some luck with. I took her advice and set up my profile and uploaded my pictures. Although the profile went up immediately, there was a 24 hour hold on the pictures while the admins reviewed them. Excited, I decided to take that time to browse around and look at some of the thousands of prospects on the site.

As I sat there scrolling through the profiles, one particular picture and profile jumped out at me. It was a picture of a gorgeous man who looked oddly familiar. I knew I had never met him before, but something about him looked very familiar, like I knew him from somewhere. His profile intrigued me even further. He wrote about having an interest in the Universe and having many unanswered questions about life. I was intrigued. I learned from his profile that he was divorced but did not have any children. Hesitantly, I sent him the equivalent of a poke. Surprisingly, even without my pictures yet being displayed, he messaged me back after reading my profile. We chatted back and forth for a few minutes via the site's messenger and then decided to talk on the phone later that night.

Even though we had a very formal first phone conversation, there was a strange, instant connection. I emailed him a picture later that night, at his request since he still had no idea what I looked like. By the next day we had both disabled our profiles. Irfan was also on rotational dating at the time. He was going to be in town in 2 weeks on business and we decided to meet then. During those 2 weeks, we spent every night talking on the phone. My mom had moved back into her home and was trying to keep upbeat while going through her chemotherapy. She noticed a change in my behavior immediately and I excitedly told her I was talking to someone that seemed like a great match. Long story short, he came in 2 weeks, and after our first dinner date, he met my family and friends the next day and proposed 2 weeks later. My parents asked for his family references, legal, and financial documents as is customary in my culture. They also spoke to his family on the phone several times before agreeing to the engagement. We were married 2 months later.

Soon afterwards my son and I moved into his home in South Carolina. I was excited to have a fresh new start in life. Things switched from the honeymoon phase to the reality and challenges that came with becoming an overnight family. I was suddenly a stay-at-home mom, away from my business, my hometown, family, and friends. All these new changes didn't come easily to me. I had been working for over 10 years and had never lived without my family. I also had no idea what it felt like to feel safe for once in my life. Functioning in fight or flight pretty much all my life had left my nervous system unable to cope with the safety and security of real love. I turned to the Law of Attraction for help, but no matter how hard I tried; I could not seem to fix my relationship with my husband. It was like we both kept triggering each other. We were two people who deeply wanted to love each other but didn't know how. I was confused.

On the surface everything was great. I had a safe home and loving partner who came home to us every evening and was very involved in the family. Somehow there was also something missing. We couldn't access each other's hearts. We both felt deeply unseen and unheard. The law of attraction has served me well so far. Why won't it work anymore, I kept asking myself. What am I missing? I kept going back to my vision board and writing down all the ways I wanted my husband to change into my ideal man. Had I made a mistake? Was this not the man I had created in my love list? I was utterly confused. The more I wanted my husband to change into this ideal version I had created in my head, the further and further he appeared to get from it.

I didn't realize this until years later, but I was having a personal identity crisis at this point in my life. Having been raised in western culture trained me to be a high achieving, independent, masculine alpha woman. Having worked since the age of 17, it felt really odd to not have my achievements and professional titles and be so dependent on my husband. Having been raised by a breadwinner mother, I had no idea what it was like to be a nurturing, caring, feminine wife and mother. These were skillsets I hadn't learned to embody. Instead of taking ownership and pride for the beautiful family we had created, I was acting like a hungry ghost trying to mine love to fill an insatiable inner void.

In March of 2010, my mother lost her battle to cancer. I felt completely lost and alone. I was 8 months pregnant and feeling completely distant from my husband. I would keep it all together during the day for my family and friends and cry myself to sleep every single night. I had lost my pillar of strength, my best friend, and my entire support system, bundled up in one amazing package, named Mom. Although surrounded by family and friends, I felt completely isolated and alone. *Someone please help me! Someone please tell me it's going to be okay.* Silence. My husband was physically there and very supportive, but for some reason we couldn't connect emotionally. 6 weeks later my son, Ayaan was born. I found some comfort in his gentle, caring, loving nature. He had this other worldly, old soul, wisdom about him from the minute I laid eyes on him. It was love at first sight. Was this baby here to save me? To help me mend through this deep gaping hole in my heart? What a huge burden and expectation I was placing on the tiny shoulders of my newborn.

When Ayaan was 18 months old, we had the opportunity to move. My husband was a consultant and traveled a lot and he wanted to be present for the kids.

He accepted a job offer in Houston, a city I always wanted to live in so I took this as a positive sign from the Universe for new beginnings. I never really felt at home in South Carolina and my husband and I jumped at the opportunity for a fresh new start. We moved to Texas in January of 2012, so I was due for a new vision board. Armed with the newness of a fresh new city, a brand new home, and new hope, I created the board with a huge focus on health, *sukoon (inner peace)*, and personal growth. Shortly after, through a series of interesting events, which I will save for some other time, I came to realize I had been living with an autoimmune disease. I had been living with Rheumatoid Arthritis, which had been chalked up to "bad genes" all these years. I vowed to cure myself from this supposedly "incurable" disease. We will talk about this more in Chapter 2.

In early 2013 as I was sitting down to redo my vision board for the year, something interesting came to my attention. *Sukoon.* This one word has been a constant from the start of my Law of Attraction journey. No matter what else was put on my vision board, I always started with the quest for inner calm and peace. In hopes of exploring this a bit further, I decided to write down why inner peace was so important to me. Through the process of writing down and playing with my thoughts on paper, I realized that without *sukoon* nothing else really mattered to me. What good was money, friends, or even the joy of motherhood if I could not enjoy it with my calm and peaceful presence? I decided to write this out as my life mission statement and make it one of my personal values. No matter what I did from this day forward, my ultimate quest was to achieve sukoon.

This discovery and mission statement had some instant positive side effects. I found myself easily able to identify the things that brought me joy and say no to all the distractions of life that didn't. No matter what everyone else was doing or buying around me, I was never tempted to "do as the Joneses" so to speak. It put all my decision making on autopilot. *Will it bring me joy? Yes! Will it waste my time without bringing any true value to my life? No, thank you.* My ultimate drive and goal in life was to do only those things that brought me inner calm and peace. Over the next few years, I found myself turning inward, digging deeper and deeper in my quest for happiness. I took off my husband's name from my vision board completely. If I wanted him to love me, I wrote down "Give Love." If I needed his attention and appreciation, I wrote "Appreciate."

I realize now that somewhere along my Law of Attraction journey, I lost track of one key ingredient, *Gratitude*. I was amazingly effective at attracting all the things I needed in my life, and undoubtedly the Universe delivered, every time. But instead of taking the time to cherish and appreciate what it had truly given me, I spent all my energy wanting everything and everyone to fit into my perfect, idealistic box. I didn't know how to truly receive all my blessings on a cellular level. I forgot to trust that the Universe knows best and had given me the best version of not only what I wanted but also what I needed.

I referred back to my love list. My husband was indeed a splitting image of everything I had ordered from the Universe. Why was I not seeing and appreciating it all these years? My first complaint was that I didn't feel loved and cherished by him. Being an introvert, he wasn't good at verbally expressing his feelings. I decided to change my perspective a bit, instead of always dwelling on everything he didn't say or do, I started keeping a log of all the things he did to show me his love. On the first day alone, my list had over 20 things on it. I sat there in awe. This man has been professing his love and affection in the only way he knew possible, by showing his love instead of just saying the right things. I could clearly see why the Universe had chosen to give me someone who showed me love over someone who merely spoke the right words. Acts of service were his love language and I had been withholding my true heartfelt appreciation all those years!

Armed with this realization, I slowly started changing my mindset and love language. Instead of thinking of all the ways my husband didn't tell me he loved me, I would focus on showing myself love. Instead of demanding his compliments and appreciation, I would sweet talk and appreciate myself. Oddly enough, once I took the spotlight off of him and switched the focus onto myself, things started changing. I was demanding he fill a void in myself that only I have the ability and permission to fill. No other person can love and appreciate me the way I wanted if I didn't love and appreciate myself. Someone with a healthy regard and love for themselves wouldn't even demand such a thing from another. They wouldn't need to. I learned quickly that once we take that pressure off of others, it opens them up to receive our love and give love in return.

Within just a few months, things started changing. I had an extra bounce in my step, I felt vibrant, energetic, and I finally felt loved. I would start my morning with going over all the things I was truly grateful for. My health, my life, my loving husband, my healthy kids, and the list went on and on. I would look in the mirror every morning, stare myself in the eyes and say, "Mina, I love you, just the way you are. Thank you for being you." I would end each day with lying in bed going over my gratitude list. I was smiling more; I was radiating some sort of an energy that came to my attention through the thousands of comments I was getting on my YouTube videos. All of a sudden, I was flooded with positive messages from people telling me my energy was contagious and they *appreciated* all my videos and positivity. I asked the Universe for appreciation, and boy I sure got it!

You see, once I was able to free my husband and the Universe of the constraints I was putting on it by demanding it do things my way, I truly unleashed the Universe to do its job. A job only the Universe knows how to do well. I kept demanding I needed appreciation from one man and one man alone, driving my husband crazy in the process, I'm sure. Once I released him from that duty, the Universe opened the door for more appreciation than I can ever phantom in one lifetime. Women were writing to me expressing their love and appreciation from every corner of the world!

Life, and husbands, have a strange way of working themselves out. The minute I started focusing on myself and letting my husband be without any demands for his attention or communication, he started doing all the things I wanted. He started communicating more verbally, he even started expressing his love and affection more. Romance was back and it was definitely here to stay. Suddenly we were back in the honeymoon phase of marriage again. A phase we had skipped over all too quickly in the first moments of our marriage. Ironically when I took the focus off of my husband and made myself the center of my own attention, I finally caught my husband's eye and affection too. Like any other relationship, things aren't perfect 100% of the time, but with the help of the Universe and proper care and affection, we keep growing and moving forward, hand in hand. As with all things worth fighting for in life, marriage and the Law of Attraction take practice with our many daily offerings to keep things moving forward.

So, what is your ultimate goal, your legacy, your life's mission? Starting from the end goal in mind really helps put things in perspective and truly live with intention. Once you have established the bigger picture of your life, all other mundane decisions will become easier to make. Your personal mission statement will guide you through life, illuminating the paths you need to take to arrive at your destination. This is an exercise I highly recommend you complete. Sit in a quiet space and put pen to paper. Invest the time in yourself to figure out what you want your legacy to be. Write it down as your personal mission statement. After this point, it will become easier to evaluate all your current commitments, priorities, and relationships. Ask yourself if your current life is in line with your mission statement. What steps can you take to become in sync with your bigger picture of life?

Expanded Edition Update:

It was so amazing to see how little my personal values have changed over time; however, how I express them now has changed and expanded. Sukoon is still my highest value and a filter I run everything through. I have become way clearer on my values and become unapologetic when it comes to owning them.

How my life has changed in this area since 2016 is this, I no longer resent my culture and eastern values. I wear them proudly and even bring that part of my heritage into my work. Healing that part of me makes me feel more whole and more connected to my deceased parents.

I am also more aware and conscious of the fact that everyone and everything is responding to me in a beautiful dynamic and ever-changing dance. My inner work has compounded on itself and I am able to do many of these processes in my mind in seconds without getting triggered. Values are such an important guidepost in life. Take some time to get clear on yours.

Affirmation:

"I am the co-creator of my reality."

Journal Prompts for Further Reflection:

If I could have it all, what would I really desire?

_____

_____

_____

If no one would be mad, and there was no right or wrong way to life, how would I live?

_____

_____

_____

What is my core personal value and mission statement?

_____

_____

_____

What do I want my life legacy to be known for?

_____

_____

_____

CHAPTER
Two
BECOME YOUR OWN DREAM GIRL ONE BITE AT A TIME

Happiness is not a destination. It is a method of life. —
Burton Hills

In my early teens I started becoming aware of some annoying health issues. I suffered many dizzy spells, had bloating issues, strange skin rashes, hair loss, premature graying, chest pain, and joint issues to name just a few. Since many of these things ran in my family, my parents and countless doctors dismissed my symptoms. In isolation, my symptoms didn't appear to be life threatening or even alarming and were often chalked up to attention seeking or other teenage issues. In my early 20s, I started noticing certain patterns. Even though my symptoms kept getting worse year by year, they would diminish if I ate very few calories a day by skipping meals. This made me make the food-health connection for the first time, although I didn't really understand it completely at this point. Over the course of an entire decade, I saw over a dozen doctors and specialists. No one knew what was wrong with me or even why I was making such a big deal out of it. During this same decade, I watched these exact symptoms get worse in my older relatives. My mom and aunts had balding spots by the time they reached the mid-30s. They were also plagued with severe joint pain that made walking even short distances a challenge. They also had weight gain, belly fat, and inflammation to the extent that it almost distorted their facial features.

My symptoms seemed to be further heightened during my first two pregnancies. Especially since I couldn't afford to miss meals when my unborn child's life was at stake. My 5'3" frame bloated an extra 65 pounds with gestational diabetes with each pregnancy making me unrecognizable to people who hadn't seen me in a while. I was so scared for my health. I didn't want to end up like my relatives. This fear worsened when my mom was suddenly diagnosed with ovarian cancer at the young age of 47. Her doctors figured her cancer had started when she was in her mid-30s. Slowly growing inside of her until her symptoms became so extreme that she needed to be hospitalized. She was gone within 2 years. A couple of years after that another one of her siblings suddenly passed away. A few years later, another one. I realized at that point that only a handful of my mother's huge family of 7 siblings had lived past the age of 55. Every single one of my relatives that passed away before their time and had suffered from the same symptoms I was dealing with. I worried I had bad genes and was doomed to end up like them. Would I not be able to watch my children grow up?

In 2012, soon after our move to Texas, the joint pain in my wrists and knees got to a point where I could no longer climb the stairs in my home. My younger son was 18 months old at the time and I couldn't lift him, open jars, or even type to reply to comments from my beloved YouTube subscribers. I would sit on the floor and let him climb onto my lap when he wanted to be carried. I had constant shoulder pain on my left side accompanied by throbbing chest pain. Since I had put health as this year's main focus on my vision board, I decided to find a new doctor and scheduled an appointment. As I waited for my appointment, I decided to go for a massage and try to alleviate some of my shoulder pain. Little did I know this massage therapist would turn out to be my guardian angel.

Before my massage even started, the therapist noticed the black spots on my back. She inquired if I had them all my life. They appeared, at least to my attention, when I was a teenager, I told her. I had been to many dermatologists over the years, but their creams never seemed to help. She then looked at the form I had filled out and noticed my notes on joint pain. "You're not a blood type O, are you?" I am. So was my mother and most of her relatives. She told me to go home after our session and look up the blood type O diet.

I went home and looked up the diet immediately. I found the decades of research done by Dr. Peter D'adamo. [4] I quickly ordered his book but meanwhile started his diet plan for type O's immediately which I found online. A major part of his plan was to eliminate gluten from my diet. Within the first 3 days, I noticed my joint pain was lessening. I could lift my baby and make my way up the stairs in our home. By the first week, the black spots on my back were gone. I felt energetic and healthy. It made sense now why my symptoms would lessen when I skipped meals. If gluten was a major issue for me, skipping meals meant not eating gluten!

By the first month, I had lost 15 pounds. All without any focus on fitness or a program catered to losing weight. It sort of just melted off. People soon started commenting on how much healthier my hair looked, something I was very sensitive to since watching my mom and aunts suffer from female baldness. In further trying to educate myself on this topic, I soon discovered a huge cult following of gluten-freers who had cured all sorts of incurable issues. I found Dr. William Davis' book, The Wheat Belly, which further increased my knowledge and reconfirmed my belief in this newfound lifestyle.[5] I contacted Dr. William Davis online and he was able to personally guide me for the first year or so of my wheat free journey.

Almost 6 weeks into my new diet, my doctor appointment came up. After running some tests, my doctor almost looked in shock as she told me I had rheu-matoid arthritis. Arthritis? But I'm only 31 years old, isn't that an old people disease? She gave me a brief lesson on autoimmune diseases and started briefing me on the medications I needed to be put on immediately. I told her I wasn't comfortable taking any medications, especially ones I would have to take forever. Medi-cations had never really suited me since I was a little child. Even simple over the counter painkillers upset my stomach and made me irritable. "You're not under-standing the seriousness of an autoimmune disease," she went on. I told her about my newly adopted gluten free lifestyle and how some of my symptoms had rap-idly decreased or completely went away. She said I had come back negative for celiac disease, but if I was no-ticing improvement, she would call a specialist friend in the field and inquire. I waited and my doctor called her friend. He explained to her I could have gotten a false negative on my celiac disease test because I had already been eating a gluten free diet. The antibodies were likely gone from my system, therefore making the test invalid. He suggested I start eating gluten again for 30 days and come back for more testing.

There was no way I was going to poison myself again just to be subjected to more testing, and then put on medication I didn't want to take! I thanked the doctor and promised her I would reconsider the med-ication and come back in two months for a follow-up. Shortly after this appointment, I was due to see a car-diologist for my chest pains. After some routine tests, I was told it was all in my head and sent home.

Armed with this new diagnosis, I dove deeper and deeper into research. I met a group of people dealing with a whole array of autoimmune diseases with similar symptoms to mine. I learned from the people taking medications that the drugs only masked symptoms momentarily and constantly needed to be upgraded to more and more powerful medications, which led to a host of new symptoms and diseases popping up in the body. It was like being caught in a never-ending cycle of drugs and disease. Some people were doing the medications along with the gluten free lifestyle, which made them only a notch above the meds only group. They yo-yoed constantly and had frequent doctor visits. Then there was the crowd that was only doing the gluten free diet or better yet, grain free lifestyle. This group appeared to be completely healthy and vibrant, living a full, rich, active life. Their symptoms only flared up when they made a bad food choice or their meals were contaminated at a restaurant or dinner party. I quickly decided I belonged in this vibrant, healed, whole group.

A year into my gluten free and medication free lifestyle, I went for my yearly physical and the doctor was surprised to learn my lifelong anemia had suddenly disappeared. My vitamin D levels had improved from dangerously low to moderate. I only had joint pain and rashes when I came in contact with gluten. "You look great!" She exclaimed. "What have you been doing? Tell me everything." I told her about the changes I had made in my diet. She took some notes and said she was going to share my experience with her family and patients.

Soon after that, some of my symptoms started to return. I mentioned this on my YouTube channel where I had been documenting my journey, and a subscriber contacted me with some advice. She told me how some of the gluten free products I was eating contained corn, which was often mistaken by the body as gluten. I cut out corn immediately and my symptoms again disappeared. Around this time, I discovered Dr. Davis' second book, Wheat Belly Total Health, which steered my journey away from processed gluten free foods and into a more naturally grain free lifestyle.[6]

Since my holistic nutrition-based journey started back in 2012, I have added another baby into our family, got down to my high school weight, and feel as young, healthy, and vibrant as ever. Nutrition has touched my heart so deeply; I have since read over 200 books and thousands of articles and research on the topic. Only 25% of the medical schools in the United States teach nutrition (of the ones that do, the average is 22.3 hours of total time spent on nutrition). According to Dr. Michael Greger, bestselling author and founder of nutritionfacts.org, "You can learn everything a properly trained doctor knows about nutrition in one long weekend."[7] Having spent 4 years studying nutrition at that point in my life, I officially considered myself more qualified than most doctors on the single most important aspect affecting human health. Pills? No thank you.

It's been over 4 years since I embarked on this journey to health and wellness at the time of writing the first edition of this book, and through proper education, many trials and errors, and emotional and physical ups and downs, I have bio hacked my body into behaving and performing at its optimal self. I have learned so many lessons along the way. Mistakes I made and things I could have done better, lessons only time and experience can teach. Through the knowledge I have gained, I now coach others battling health and wellness issues though their journeys. Everything I have learned can't be summed up into this book, but there are some key things I would like to point out.

Through my research, I made an important discovery that really helped shift my mindset from a passive victim of my genes to an active participant in my health. I learned that through certain lifestyle choices, we have the ability to turn on or off specific genes, this is known as epigenetics. As it turns out, our genes account for a very small percentage of our overall health and wellness. It only appears to have a larger correlation for several reasons. Mainly due to the fact that we are likely to repeat the mistakes of our parents and even earlier ancestors through damaging lifestyle habits learned and repeated generation after generation.

According to Dr. Frank Lipman, Founder of Eleven Eleven Wellness Center, "[…] unchangeable, unmodifiable genes represent less than 2 percent of our genetic makeup. Most of our genes are actually modifiable and can be turned on or off. In fact, you are changing your genetics daily and perhaps even hourly from the foods you eat, the air you breathe and even by the thoughts you think."[8] This information was truly a huge motivator and game changer for me. I now had some hope and control over my health instead of being doomed by my genes.

The single most important thing you can take away from my experience is this: don't blindly trust what a man or woman in a white coat tells you. Be proactive. Ask questions. You always have the option to walk away and do more research before you agree to take any medications. This doesn't mean walking away and asking another poorly trained, burnt out, eager to get you out the door doctor for a second opinion to the same medical school trained protocol. Do your due diligence, seek out advice from others that may have the same issues, read books, join forums, find studies, and seek out alternatives. Your ultimate goal should be optimal health and wellness, not simply masking symptoms so you can get through another day. You play a key, active role in your wellbeing. You can't just leave that on the hands of the first name that pops up in your health insurance directory.

I'm not saying doctors don't have a place in our lives. They come in pretty handy when we fall off our bike and break our arm, are in a traffic accident, or are the victims of a gunshot or stab wound. An immediate serious threat definitely calls for medical attention. A doctor however, no matter how qualified, can't out treat your poor nutritional choices. He or she can merely suppress your symptoms by trying to trick your brain with pharmaceuticals. Fortunately, your body has a natural healing ability built into it and perfected over millions of years of evolution that can't be tricked. Only you have the power to unleash its natural ability to heal through your lifestyle choices.

Nutrition plays a key role in resetting the damage our lifestyle choices and environment has done to our bodies. We can achieve this by reverting back to a diet our species has evolved to eat over the slow process of millions of years. Unfortunately, we have changed our lifestyle and environment so rapidly over the last few centuries, evolution hasn't had time to catch up with us. We are sicker than ever. Our illnesses and excess weight deform our bodies and slowly rot our brains with diseases our ancestors couldn't even dream of. We are walking around with all sorts of anxiety and mental disorders and have no clue as to why the pills we keep popping aren't helping.

Author of The Paleo Manifesto, John Durant, who studied evolutionary psychology at Harvard under Steven Pinker, says that when an animal kept in zoo captivity falls ill, we turn to the wild to see how that species eats and behaves and try to replicate that environment in the zoo. The best way to learn how any species eats or behaves is to observe it in its natural habitat. Since the way most of us live now is far from the human species' natural habitat, we turn to our ancestors to see how they lived and ate. It can be summed up in this: Eat lots of vegetables, some fruits, nuts, seeds, lean meats if you choose to, and avoid gluten.

Wheat, a primary source of gluten, was introduced into the human diet only about 10,000 years ago.[9] From an evolutionary perspective, that is not enough time for us to adapt to it. Stay as far away as possible from processed foods that have been artificially made and are loaded with toxins and chemicals. The truth is there are many toxins and chemicals in our environment today that we simply can't avoid. We can, however, minimize our exposure by eliminating toxins from our foods as much as possible. By focusing on the things that we do have the power of controlling, we lessen the overall impact and load these foreign substances placed on our bodies.

A natural diet of clean, whole, mostly natural foods takes some getting used to if you are the typical person addicted to the standard American diet (SAD). There is a reason you are addicted to these foods. They are loaded with chemicals and additives engineered to have drug-like effects on our brains. These food-like products are formulated to get us addicted, increase our cravings and overall appetite. This makes it nearly impossible to break the cycle no matter how much we want to change. Here is where the "everything in moderation" rule fails for so many. When we keep re-introducing these foods into our system, even in small amounts, we keep appetite-increasing addictive chemicals in our system, always wanting us to keep coming back for more. I know it's hard, but it really is best to remove these food-like products from our lives altogether. If it was easy, everyone would be doing it, but since it isn't, if you can adopt this life-style change, you can stand out from the crowd.

I believe in going for the high hanging fruit. If you only adopt one thing from this book, make it this. I promise you, even the people who think your eating habits are strange will be asking you what you have been doing to look so fabulous. People ask me all the time how I lost weight or why I look years younger than my age. When I start listing all the things I do, they almost always look disappointed, hoping I could just recommend a pill or quick fix drink. Sorry, I don't have a pill or potion you can take. You're going to have to do it the old-fashioned way. This is the way millions of humans before us have stayed fit, healthy, and fabulous, shaping our evolution, biochemistry and history in the process.

Dr. David Perlmutter, medical doctor and author of books, Grain Brain and Brain Maker, brings some ground breaking research to our attention. According to the latest research "[...] up to 90 percent of all known human illnesses can be traced back to an unhealthy gut." Our microbiome, a collection of unique and complex microorganisms living in our bodies, "[...] affects our mood, libido, metabolism, immunity, and even our perception of the world and the clarity of our thoughts." Basically, everything about you, how you feel, your outlook of the world, the energy you have or lack, and whether you are fat or thin, is directly linked to the friendly bacteria in your gut. According to Dr. Perlmutter, the bugs in your gut might as well have been classified as an organ because of their overall impact and function in our bodies. As much as 80 to 90 percent of the feel-good hormone, Serotonin, is produced in the gut! The damaging foods and medications we take, disrupts our gut's bacteria, causing inflammation in our bodies and brains, which has been directly linked to depression. In studies where scientists have injected completely healthy individuals with a substance to cause inflammation, they instantly develop signs of depression![10] If this isn't reason enough to change our eating habits, I don't know what is.

When you eat for optimal health and beauty and don't suppress the body's natural communication systems with unnecessary medications like pain killers, antidepressants, or chemicals found in modern food-like products; you will open up clear lines of communication with your body. When you eat something that causes a headache, you'll learn not to eat it again or at the very least limit its consumption. In turn your body will be fully alert and ready to use its resources to fight off illnesses and ailments. Your hair will grow, your skin will radiate, and you will suddenly have all the energy you desire to live your best life moving forward. Changing your nutrition is the single best and easiest way to transform your health, wellbeing, beauty and your life.

Expanded Edition Update:

At 42 years of age, I feel younger, look better, and have more energy than I ever had in my life! Even better than my 20s. I have my younger self to thank for that. Eating the way I was eating at that time in my life shaped my identity and created lifelong good habits. I still eat a very low carb, mostly carnivore diet. I have eliminated the green smoothies I used to drink and focus on getting most of my calories from protein. Nutrition is still my main health, wellness, and beauty plan and so far, I seem to be very happy and content with it. I have since quit caffeine and that has doubled my energy.

Since writing the first edition, my husband and children have also adapted this way of eating. My husband eats a mostly low carb carnivore diet and Armaan is definitely the only carnivore and the strictest out of all of us. Currently we live in a very fun and vibrant neighborhood full of exciting restaurants and new ones popping up daily. To celebrate the foodie and fun part of us we enjoy treats here and there but always make up for it through Intermittent Fasting. Fasting has many health benefits and something I have been enjoying for over a decade now. I highly suggest you look into fasting and adding it to your regimen after consulting your doctor.

Homework:

I recommend keeping a food journal for a week and writing down how you feel in your body and the accompanying moods before, during, and a few hours after meals. This will give you a more holistic view of how certain foods react with your body.

JOURNAL PROMPTS FOR FURTHER REFLECTION

Are the foods I am eating serving my future self?

_____

_____

_____

How do I feel in my body and mind before and after eating?

_____

_____

_____

Does the pleasure from my meals last for hours or does it turn into discomfort?

_____

_____

_____

CHAPTER
Three
FIT GIRL ERA

Those who think they have no time for bodily exercises will sooner or later have to find time for illness. — Edward Stanley

B elieve it or not, exercise played a small role in my overall health transformation. I think many people make the mistake of starting here. Yes, I just called starting an exercise program first a mistake! When your nutrition is all out of whack, and you're drugging up your body in a desperate attempt to shut up its many cries for help, what will an exercise regimen do for you really? We start some sort of a sad fitness regimen, see no change in the first few days, and then we quit. This process actually disappoints our internal audience, making us lose respect and self-esteem for ourselves! That's how the vicious cycle continues. When you're putting the entire burden of your transformation on a couple of treadmill runs, you're bound to fail. I don't view exercise as the main component to my health journey. A total change in mindset was needed for me to realize that exercise alone will not give me health and the body of my dreams. The truth is, unless you're an actual celebrated elite athlete, your nutrition makes the single most impact on your weight and health, not exercise. Exercise has many health and mood boosting benefits and should be part of your daily routine for only those reasons. It should not carry the burden of major weight loss or undoing your poor eating habits.

In my previous life, after the birth of my first child, I hired a personal trainer to lose the excess 50 pounds I was left with. I would spend 4-5 hours a week doing grueling workout routines but saw little difference in my body. I eventually did lose that weight, but it came only after I changed my diet. After having two more babies since then and having to lose another collective 120 pounds, I finally learned something I wish I knew sooner. If your nutrition is on point, you need very little exercise to maintain a bombshell figure. That's why I eventually stopped going to my workouts with the trainer. Even after spending thousands of dollars and countless hours at the gym, it brought me little joy or pleasure to work out. It took me exactly 10 years to find a fitness regimen that I enjoyed. In April 2015, when I had already improved many areas of my life, fixed my relationship, had a happy, healthy body, family, and home, I decided it was time to add that one missing piece into my life.

As I do with everything, I started reading books, blogs, research, and watching YouTube videos on my quest for finding my personal fitness program. I realized quickly that a lot of the conventional advice said conflicting things. There were hundreds of conflicting studies supporting both sides of the fitness wars. I therefore came to the conclusion that there really was no perfect way to workout, only *perfect for you*.

I started testing out the various programs, beach body, cardio only, weights only, Kayla Itsines' plans, and a weights and cardio combo. Soon realizing that I was seeing results no matter what program I was following, since my diet was so on point. It didn't even matter whether I was working out for 20 minutes a day or 90 minutes a day. I quickly narrowed it down to which program I truly enjoyed and actually looked forward to doing. For me it ended up being a weight lifting only program that I could do at home. Not only do I enjoy this program and look forward to my 5 workouts a week, but I only need to do 20-30 minutes of training to see massive results. This is because I'm working out for enjoyment and for my overall health and wellness. There is no pressure on my workouts to help me out train an outrageous diet or lose massive amounts of weight.

Now I'm not saying you can't lose weight by working out alone, without little or no change to your diet. Any change in the right direction will bring some results, but it's much more work to do it this way. In my testing phase, when I tried the cardio only routine, I was not only moody and irritable for hours afterwards, but I wanted to eat everything in sight. Cardio just seemed to unleash my hunger out of control, undoing all my effects in the gym. I didn't have that effect when lifting weights. My advice is to try out many different programs and find one that works for you. Something you can do in a short amount of time and that brings you joy, making it so much easier to stick with. Definitely get your nutrition in check first. Starting both a new nutrition plan and fitness regimen at the same time is challenging and you are more likely to fall off the wagon.

I have had much success in having my clients change their nutrition first and lose the bulk of the weight before they ease into a fitness program they enjoy. Good eating habits take much of the pressure off of exercise and you have to work out so much less to see results. I also find that when you disconnect the fitness and "diet" parts as separate phases instead of doing it as one plan, you are less likely to reward yourself with food after your workouts. Unlinking food and fitness somehow tricks your brain into putting an equal effort into both of them. When you do both together at the same time, you are always eating to reward yourself after a "good" workout, or working out extra hard trying to undo that "bad" weekend of unhealthy eating. It's best to see them as completely separate parts of your overall pie. They are not partners in crime.

In the first few months of starting my exercise regimen, I was actually gaining weight. Had I started working out before I implemented the nutritional changes, I would have freaked out and stopped working out for sure. I personally believe there is no one right way to exercise. Take the time to find something you love to do. Do it 3-6 times a week, 20-30 minutes at a time, unless of course you enjoy doing more. That's all you need to maintain a lovely figure if your nutrition is up to par. When you add a little bit of movement to a powerhouse of nutrition, the body's natural weight regulation system will take care of the rest and maintain its ideal weight.

Some people thrive in fitness classes, others are gym bunnies, while others hate the thought of having to exercise in public. For my family, it made sense to build a small home gym. My husband and son both share the gym with me so the cost was equivalent to a 1 years' worth of family membership at our local gym. The home gym more than paid for itself in the first year. We don't have to leave the house to get in a quick workout every morning. Rain or sunshine, it gets done. Find what works for you and stick with it.

Even if you end up getting a gym membership or enroll in group fitness classes, have a plan B for home. Set up a small area in your home as your backup workout plan. Use this space to get in a quick workout if you don't have time to make it to the gym for whatever reason. Bad weather? Sick child? No excuse, you can still get a quick workout at home. This keeps you in the habit of working out and forms your identity. When we miss one workout, it's so much easier to miss more. Missing a workout here and there may seem harmless, but before you know it, it's not so much a habit anymore.

Having a workout plan is awesome, but you also need to find other ways to move your body. If you work out for an entire hour but sit for the remaining 23, you are not in optimal health. The body was not designed to sit for long hours like the average person does these days. You need to realize there are many more ways to move your body than the actual act of fitness or working out. Make a conscious decision to not sit all the time. I love watching YouTube videos and would easily sit and watch 1-2 hours' worth in one sitting. This was not good for my body or for time management. I decided I can cure both issues by only watching YouTube while standing up or walking. This not only got me up and moving, but it drastically cut down on my viewing time. Who has time to stand around all day right?

Learn to find new ways to move more even if it's at a slow pace. Meet your girlfriends for a walk instead of the usual lunch or coffee date. Good for your health and your wallet. The bottom line is to get up and get moving. Stop sitting around talking about how you plan to start working out for 2 hours every day. You won't do it and you really have no reason to work out for that long. Do short, efficient workouts that you enjoy. Find ways outside of exercise to NOT sit for long stretches of time.

Expanded Edition Update:

I am still working out pretty much the same way I was when I wrote this chapter. The things I shared in this book really have been my consistent structures and containers that allowed me to quantum leap! Here are the few things I have changed. My home gym is now a bit bigger and better and includes a red-light therapy section as well as an infrared sauna, both of which I absolutely love using. Earlier this year I took up Pilates and had joined a studio with some personal training sessions. After about a month, I added what I had learned into my existing home workout and didn't need the studio.

Currently I do red light therapy for about 15 minutes a session, followed by 10 minutes on my vibration plate, then lift weights for about 20 minutes, 4-5 times a week. Followed by about 25 minutes in the sauna. I love listening to books on audible while working out. This is my current perfect routine and makes me feel and look great.

Fitness is one of the most undervalued beauty and lifestyle hacks. Having a fit, toned body instantly puts you in the top 1%. You feel and look decades younger and people also make some very positive assumptions about your confidence and discipline levels on a subconscious level. If you really want an upper hand in life, start a fitness routine today and stick to it for the rest of your life. Your future self will thank you like I am thanking that younger version of myself today!

Affirmations:

"My body is my temple."

"Caring for myself makes me feel loved and adored."

Journal Prompts for Further Reflection

Am I currently happy with my body shape and tone? What does my dream shape look and feel like?

_____

_____

_____

What kind of a short, fun workout can I commit to for the next 60 days?

_____

_____

_____

How can I make my new routine satisfactory with my internal audience so it can cheer me on instead of putting me down?

_____

_____

_____

CHAPTER
Four
ONE CONFRONTATION AWAY FROM LEVEL 10 CRAY

Stress is nothing more than a socially acceptable form of mental illness.
-Richard Carlson

Motherhood has many sleepless nights. There really is no way around this. I have spent what seems like huge chunks of my life in a sleepless zombie-like stage as I nursed my babies and rocked and cuddled them for hours through the night. Once that stage is over and sleep once again becomes a part of reality and not just a distant dream, I feel like a normal person again. My diet improves, concentration becomes sharper, energy returns, and I have been suddenly reborn. I am no longer one confrontation away from a crazy mess of hormones. It probably didn't help that all 3 of my kids are spaced apart and I had to start over again with each one. Life becomes glorious again. During all three of the baby stages of my children's lives, I ran into that group of women who have the option of sleeping but stay up watching TV or surfing the net instead. They complain of not having the energy or motivation they need to get things done, having cravings for unhealthy foods throughout the day, and a host of other health issues. Why someone would deliberately want to mess with their sleep, jeopardizing their health, beauty, and overall quality of life is utterly outside of the scope of my understanding.

The term beauty sleep exists for a reason, and I personally wouldn't play around with my health and beauty. Aim to get at least 7-8 hours of sleep every night. Nothing is more important than your health and sanity. Just a few nights of restful sleep can change your entire perspective and outlook on life. You suddenly have the energy for intimacy with your partner, exercise, better control over your cravings, and clarity of mind and better decision-making skills. Dr. Sara Gottfried, MD and author of The Hormone Reset Diet, says "mastering your sleep is one of the smartest ways of regulating your hormones." It turns out that nearly every hormone is released in response to your sleep/wake cycles. Getting a restful night's sleep signals our body on how much cortisol to release in our system. This stress hormone controls how we behave throughout the rest of the day. How much energy we have, how much we eat, and how we handle stressful situations. Cortisol also affects our thyroid, and can slow it down, causing weight gain, among a host of other very serious health problems.[11]

One of the most important things you can do is having a nightly bedtime routine for both you and your children. We start winding down cleaning up around 7 pm every evening. By 8 pm the kids are ready for bed and starting to settle into their rooms. My husband and I take care of the final kitchen and living room pickup and are in bed by 8:30 pm. We take a couple of hours to spend time with each other without the distractions of kids. This is our time to invest into the marriage, talking, watching movies, or life and financial planning. By 10:30 we are asleep. Keeping this schedule has been very effective for my family since we have a ritualistic process that our bodies have adapted to. When your entire family is rested, they are ready to take on the many responsibilities and challenges of the day with grace. This may not work for everyone, but retreating to our rooms early in the evening helps my husband and I have some alone time and invest into our relationship, and it also shows the kids that sleep is important to us too. They need to see that we are not sending them away while we are partying downstairs.

There will always be one more show to watch, one last Facebook chat session with a friend, or one more text message, but there is only one of you. If you don't care for and nurture your health and beauty, you will quickly let it get away from you. Prevention is always easier than having to find a cure when life is really a mess. If you have a spouse or other family members that don't share your dreams of getting a restful night of sleep, show them by example. We can't control other people, but we can certainly inspire them by making changes in our own behavior. Get your rest, wake up with energy and zest in the morning and let them slowly realize how amazing you look and feel after a good night's sleep. Without any criticism or demand for change in anyone else's behavior, your actions will inspire them to make changes for themselves. Trust me when you lead with example, people notice.

Although sleep will help regulate your cortisol and in turn affect your stress responses, there is still more you can do to alleviate unnecessary stress in your life. If you remember, in Chapter 1 we talked about the importance of having a big picture mission statement for your life. Once you have taken the time to develop yours, you will need to evaluate and make the necessary changes in your life to become more in sync with that statement. Does your current schedule, obligations, commitments, living arrangements, friends, family, and even relationships fit your mission statement? I have had to take this step many times in my life. Some relationships and friendships were painful to let go of, but they were honestly the best investment I made in my personal growth and wellbeing. Hanging on to people, relationships, and things that no longer served me well, burdened my life, and didn't fit into my values of not owning and being owned by other people. The process of letting go has been the most liberating and freeing process of my journey to personal development.

You will learn through this process that much of what we do in our lives is the result of what we think others want us to do. We want to fit in and be accepted, that is part of our human history and evolution. This is where choosing the right friends and social circles serves us well. We ultimately become who we hang out with, whether you can admit to that or not. As the old saying goes, misery loves company. By changing your behavior, they feed their own insecurities. Surround yourself instead with people who are in line with your personal values and goals. A group of like-minded friends will keep you in check as you inspire each other in staying true to your life's missions. Even if it means having less friends, I would much rather choose quality over quantity any day. When you are fully present and aware of your path, you attract the right type of people into your life.

Letting go of commitments that don't bring us joy is another important step in our stress management. Parties with people we dislike, events we sign up for that drain our time and energy, and the many activities we sign our kids up for to keep up with their friends. What a waste of time, money, and effort, and you're teaching your kids that there is more value in keeping up with others than in staying true to your own belief systems. Learn to say no thank you, and move on.

Even if we follow all these steps, not all stress can be avoided. There will always be deadlines at work, situations with kids, and traffic jams to deal with. This is where having a healthy positive mindset will serve you well. Not every situation is in your control, but how you react and deal with the situation is always in your control.

I had an incident when I was 8 months pregnant with my first child. Running late for a client meeting and wanting to pick up a sandwich on the way, I was really annoyed when my best friend called me on the home phone. She was so excited and sharing a story with me, and all I could think about was getting off the phone with her to rush out the door. After what seemed like 15 minutes of eternity, I finally told her I would call her after my meeting and dashed out the door. On route to the sandwich place, I encountered a traffic jam and sirens from all sorts of police and emergency vehicles. Come to find out, a car had driven through the restaurant, killing several people on the spot and injuring others. Had I not gotten that call from my friend, I would have been in the place at exactly the time it was struck with the car. From that day on, I never get upset if a situation or plans change, even if I'm stuck in a traffic jam or miss an important event.

You never know what the Universe is saving you from. Change your mindset and you will instantly change your stress level. When a stressful situation arises, you have the option of saying, "that was annoying, but you must have something better in store for me. I trust your judgment."

Simplify your life to the point of getting the most value out of each item you devote yourself to. As a culture we need to learn that it's okay, desirable even, to have some free time. It's okay to be bored. It's okay to have some unscheduled time with absolutely nothing to do. It's crucial for our health as this has been a major part of our human history and evolution. When you take out the garbage, you have more time to be fully present for the things that do matter and bring you joy. We will explore this more in the upcoming chapters. This is so crucial to your wellbeing that I have broken it down further into small, manageable steps.

Expanded Edition Update:

OMG, so this chapter was probably my biggest jump. I now have older kids who finally sleep through the night in their own rooms. For the first time in my life, I get to sleep 8 hours straight in one stretch every night and feel like a completely new person! I also no longer manifest people or situations that stress me out.

I have better boundaries around my time and energy and also reserve more of an observer's stance in most things in life. Staying in solution consciousness versus problem consciousness has also been a huge gamechanger. In my fight or flight stage, before inner work, my mind used to invent imagery problems and then spend hours trying to solve things that hadn't actually occurred. Needless to say, I no longer solve problems that haven't occurred yet. I have upgraded what I consider a problem in my life and the standard is very high!

Affirmation:

"Everything is always working out for me."

Journal Prompts for Further Reflection:

Do you feel rested every morning? What is your night time routine like? Are you feeling satisfied with the amount of sleep that you are getting?

What do you need to let go of to get more sleep? How will this tradeoff be worth it to you?

CHAPTER
Five
GET OFF OF ME

One way to organize your thoughts is to tidy up, even if it's in places where it makes no sense at all. -Ursus Wehrli

A huge part of stress management is reorganizing your life, belongings, home, and social circles in a way that they serve and bring you joy. If you are constantly looking for things, having trouble keeping up with chores, or dreading your social commitments, it's time to reorganize your life. Although my husband and I thought we were pretty organized and conscious of what we buy and bring into our home, it turns out we had much room for improvement. We recently discovered the Marie Kondo method through her life changing book, "The life changing magic of tidying up."[12] We were both blown away and inspired by her technique. We spent a whole month carefully combing through our entire home, top to bottom, purging bags and bags of items that no longer served us. Goes to show you that there really is always room for improvement, no matter how much we think we have it under control. We sold stuff, donated, gifted, and yes, even trashed what seemed like thousands of belongings that we were hanging on to. Not only did our whole environment suddenly change and feel lighter and more manageable, we instantly felt happier and more content. We were left with a clean, efficient home where each item serves a purpose and brings us joy. I highly recommend her method and suggest you take the time to reclaim your environment.

There were several immediate results of our editing and purging every corner of our home. Since we got to see, all at once, the bags and bags of items we had accumulated that served no purpose in our lives; it made us question our spending habits. Why did we really have all this stuff that we obviously didn't use or need? We instantly became more conscious consumers and shopping no longer seemed like a desirable pastime.

Secondly, it became so much easier to clean and maintain my home. So much so that we no longer needed to hire a maid. Without clutter and random knick-knacks, I finally achieved my dream of having clean, item-less countertops. Things became easier to locate and put back in place for my entire family, including my 2-year-old. Every item had a place and a purpose. Getting ready was a breeze in the morning now that our wardrobes only contained items that not only fit but were also things we adored and loved wearing. Everyone instantly seemed better rested, put together, and less stressed out.

Redo each room in your home and office so that it serves the purpose you have intended for it. The kitchen should be a sanctuary for creating nurturing, healthy foods. Remove distractions, clutter, and foods you shouldn't be eating. Why dangle a Snickers bar in front of your face, hoping you can keep your will-power? Get rid of it. Your closet should be clean and organized in a way that best serves getting dressed in the morning efficiently. It should only contain items you love to wear and that flatter your figure. Bedrooms should be sanctuaries for romance and sleep. Clutter free, neat, and well-organized surroundings drastically reduce anxiety and make cleaning up a breeze. Try it, it's truly life changing.

The same goes for people in our lives that we may have been hanging on to. Friends that are a drain on our time and energy but we keep up with because of our history together. Not only are they bringing you down with their constant barrage of negative energy and need for validation, but they are taking up precious time and energy that you will never get back. That time and energy could have been allocated towards nurturing the relationships and investments that matter to us most. By hanging on to these friendships, we are also doing these people injustice. We lead them on a path where we are no longer fully present and invested. By freeing them, you are liberating yourself and helping them find people that better serve their emotional needs.

Social media can also be a huge drain on our moods. I am quick to unfollow people who constantly post negative or disturbing news stories. There is no good that comes from surrounding yourself with things that bring your soul down. I follow only happy, mood boosting sites that post uplifting, inspiring things. I believe it was Mother Teresa, who when invited to an antiwar rally, declined politely by saying, "If there is ever a peace rally, invite me." Focusing on fighting cancer creates more cancer, watching videos on dying starving children brings you down and does absolutely nothing for those children. If you want to make a difference, do something about it close to home. Sharing videos and negative posts on Facebook while sitting in your cushy home helps no one. Volunteer or donate in your local community. Charity always begins at home. You can remain Facebook friends but unfollow people's negative social media feeds. Your job is to keep yourself happy, sane, and healthy for your spouse and children. Everything else comes second.

Truthfully speaking, I do sometimes have moments where I doubt letting go of long-standing friendships that no longer brought me joy and held me back in many ways. The human brain, you see, works in funny ways. When we are distant from someone for a while, we seem to remember them in a more positive light than they actually were. In my younger years, every time I attempted to rekindle an old friendship I had consciously moved away from, I would be quickly reminded of why I had left them in the first place! Trust your instincts and your gut feelings on things. It's true that sometimes people change and grow and can make it work a second time around, but it's rare.

If certain people in your life trigger you, this may be a sign that you need some distance. Triggers are emotional wounds, very similar to physical wounds. If someone brushes up against them, we feel pain. What they said or did to cause that pain is known as a trigger. Some people trigger us accidently, while others trigger us purposely because they can see it gets under our skin. This will keep showing up in your life until you take time to heal. I decided to take some distance from people in both categories to do some healing work. They had already revealed to me what my triggers were, so their job was done. Imagine someone keeps scraping up a physical wound while you are trying to heal it. Your agendas would collide. Taking time away freed up emotional energy for me to heal my emotional wounds without someone constantly scraping them up.

Expanded Edition Update:

I protect my emotional energy now more than ever and am conscious of when and where mine is being invested. Having learned that not everyone is meant to come with us into every phase of our journey, I'm quicker to release people with love and light. I effortlessly allow all those that don't serve me to deselect and find their own true voice and higher calling. Focusing my energy into only those people, places, and things that align with my highest values has served me well and is something I continue to practice and embody.

A few years ago, I discovered Human Design through a couple of my students. Learning about the energy types and the fact that I am a Projector brought so many things into perspective and expanded my understanding about my unique energetic needs. Before Human Design, I was never really into personality types or even astrology much because I felt people were using it to limit themselves. However, even for someone like me, Human Design has been such a huge validation and blueprint on how to best use my waves of energy.

If you haven't yet, I highly recommend looking up your Human Design chart online. If you need help reading your chart, I recommend contacting my son Armaan for an in-depth reading. The open centers in my chart mean I need to take steps to empty out my centers if I come in contact with energy I don't want to amplify. I felt very seen and validated after discovering this energetic blueprint.

Homework:

For Human Design Readings, contact Armaan at

majestyofdivinity@gmail.com.

Affirmation:

"I use my energy efficiently and consciously in aligned ways."

JOURNAL PROMPTS FOR REFLECTION:

How does your home environment make you feel? Is there room for improvement?

_____

_____

_____

If you had to remove 80% of the outdated and only take 20% of your stuff into a new upgraded identity, what would that look like?

_____

_____

_____

Are certain friendships holding you back in life?

_____

_____

_____

Who could you be if you didn't have to waste so much emotional energy on that relationship?

_____

_____

_____

What are some emotional triggers you need to heal?

_____

_____

_____

CHAPTER
Six
ADULTING

*"Our life is frittered away by detail. Simplify, simplify, simplify!
I say, let your affairs be as two or three, and not a hundred or
a thousand; instead of a million count half a dozen, and keep
your accounts on your thumb-nail."*
-Henry David Thoreau

Time management is my number one secret weapon to success and balance between work and family life. Without proper time management you really can't find the time to do anything else, can you? Time is our greatest asset, yet we waste it on useless, unfulfilling, mundane tasks without giving it a second thought. If you can learn to better manage and allocate your time to serve your needs, you will suddenly achieve all that you desire. I have come to learn that it takes more energy and time to complain and worry about doing something than to actually complete the task. Every evening before going to bed, I spend a couple of minutes organizing and allocating my time for the next day. I write my two most important tasks as the first two things I need to do. Everything else comes after that. I spend the most time and effort in doing the first two things and then if time is left, I will get to the others. Knowing how my day is structured prevents me from having anxiety about all the things that need to get done. According to bestselling author and motivational speaker, Brian Tracy, you will never get caught up on everything that needs to get done. There will always be new things added to your never-ending tasks and to do lists. Learn to focus and shift your attention to your most important tasks first.[13] Wake up every morning and instead of thinking about all the stuff you have to do, attack those two things first. Then whether you get to the others or not, at least you have your most important tasks out of the way.

As mothers, I understand that there are many daily mundane, urgent and non-urgent tasks we have to do. Through much trial and error, I have found a system that works for me. I schedule the many things that I don't necessarily enjoy but need to get done, cleaning my home, laundry, etc. It helps so much to know that laundry will get done on Sunday afternoon and Monday evenings is cleaning day. That way I am not constantly distracted or anxious about getting to these tasks, which helps me focus all my energy on the most important and enjoyable tasks. Putting mundane tasks on auto pilot has proven to be a huge success and game changer in managing my business and my family life.

Get in the habit of preparing for the day ahead of time. Take a few minutes the night before to choose and set aside outfits for the next day. Write down your two most important tasks. I have gotten my sons in the habit of doing this as well. Saves so much time on school mornings when they already have their outfits picked out and know their two most important tasks when they get home from school. Once that habit is established, it puts almost everything on autopilot. An immediate result of this for my entire family was a sense of calm and peace which resulted in more creativity and efficiency in our lives. Not wasting precious time and energy on mundane tasks lets us focus on the things that really matter and bring us success. It's no wonder some of the greatest innovators, thought leaders, and highly successful people wear a daily uniform to work! Steve Jobs, Mark Zuckerberg, and President Obama are some of the many successful people who wear the same thing eliminating what is known as decision fatigue. When we spend too much time making frequent, irrelevant decisions, it keeps us from being able to make more important decisions later.[14]

Obviously, you know that fashion and looking and feeling good is important to me. I can't go as extreme as wearing the same thing, but I have been able to apply this concept into my life. We will explore my wardrobe in greater detail in chapter 9, but it's important to mention it here as it greatly affects time management. Simplify all the mundane decisions and tasks that need to be completed and you will turbocharge your brain to be more creative on the aspects of your life where it truly matters. Personally, I have noticed much less anxiety, clarity of mind, contentment in all areas of my life, clear focus, and ability to think creatively and out-side the box. All from simplifying and reorganizing my life so that my greatest efforts are spent on the things that really matter most to me.

My husband introduced the concept of like, dislike, and neutral energy regarding household tasks and it was a game changer for us! Here is how we made it work. We made a list of all the household things that need to be done on a daily, weekly, or monthly basis and who was able to do them in our family. Then we took a quick poll to see if we each liked the task, disliked it, or if it was neutral. As an example, lawn mowing is something that needs to be done every 2 weeks, my husband is the only one that can do it, and he dislikes it. So that needs to be outsourced. We decided that no one should be doing things they disliked, especially if someone else is neutral in that area or if it's easy to hire someone else to do it. We assigned tasks based on who likes doing them or at least was neutral and it felt so good! I later started using the same principle in my business and it worked equally well. It helps me stay in my zone of genius while letting the people around me thrive in theirs.

Sometimes as women we can get into our head about no one else being capable enough to do the things we do well. We feel they won't do it as well as us and it will require even more effort to "fix it" than to do it all our-selves in the first place. This is usually a sign that you have trouble receiving help. Seeing others as capable has been a game changer in my life. See them as capable and accept that they may have different ways of doing things and this doesn't necessarily mean one way or better than the other. Doing it all yourself breeds resentment and also makes you feel alone and unloved. Learn to accept help and let go of things that cause unnecessary friction in your life.

Expanded Edition Update:

I really appreciate the fact that I kept my life very simple during those early formative years of my babies' lives. That season of life required me to be as minimalistic and simple in my life to focus on the most important things. As you will learn in the last chapter of this expanded edition, I was using my masculine energy to manage time as most people do when I wrote the original chapter. I still keep my priorities straight and don't take on too many things. Since then, I have activated so much more of my feminine energy. Feminine energy has this element of timelessness that puts us in flow. Once in flow, you no longer function in linear time and instead collapse time and achieve so much more with much less effort. In feminine energy things move slower, feel way more nourishing in our bodies, and yet have much bigger effects on what we want to create.

I am also better and quicker to recognize things that need to be automated or delegated. I trust that there are people around me who want to support me and love doing the things that I may not enjoy doing. I now have a small team supporting me in both my business and my home. I may have been going faster by myself but can definitely go further with support.

Affirmation:

"It feels so good to be divinely supported."

JOURNAL PROMPTS
FOR REFLECTION:

What tasks do you like, dislike or feel neutral about?
Are there people you can find who love doing what
you dislike?

_____

_____

_____

How can you see others as capable and delegate some
of these tasks?

_____

_____

_____

Is doing everything yourself causing resentments and
exhaustion in your life?

_____

_____

_____

CHAPTER
Seven
UNBOTHERED

"Promise me Mina that you will always take care of yourself. Put yourself first so you don't end up like me." -Sheena (My mother's last words to me)

I f you remember, in the very beginning of this book, we discussed our internal audience, a term coined by Dr. Doug Lisle, to describe an imaginary audience in our head that mimics the people we want to most impress in our lives. This audience takes on the essence of those people and gives us feedback based on the many rehearsals we do in private. Since we don't want our actual friends and colleagues seeing us rehearse, we have the internal audience that gives us feedback on how we are doing. Dr. Lisle describes how it's easy to take control of this internal audience mechanism simply by rehearsing more diligently in the areas we need to improve. Impressing our internal audience raises our self-esteem, which in turn makes us care less about what others actually think about us. It's almost ironic since this mechanism came to exist through millions of years of evolution so that we could make the right decisions when it came to impressing our clans, tribes, or communities, which increased our rate of survival. As long as we make a diligent effort to impress our internal audience, our self-esteem will continue to rise, and it will matter less and less what others actually think of us. It's like having your own inner mafia! Learn to feed the beast and you will thrive!

I have firsthand experienced this in my life and can attest to it. The more effort and inner work I do on myself, eating right, working out, spending time nurturing my soul and passions, the stronger and more unbreakable and unbothered I feel. This has in turn made me focus less and less on what others are thinking of me or how they expect me to behave. I can now stay true to myself and live the life I want to live without worrying about how others want me to live.

Living authentically has been a truly freeing and liberating feeling. Surprisingly enough, the more I am true to myself, the more the right type of people are attracted into my life. I say the right type of people, because it's important to realize that not everyone can handle others living authentically. I honestly feel this makes people uncomfortable because it forces them to look in the mirror and reevaluate how they may be living. You will see some of these people fall out of your circle of friends. Don't fret, because so many others will suddenly be attracted towards your radiance and happiness. True lit from within joy is a very powerful magnet. It attracts people to you through a very powerful force, even if they have no idea why they may be drawn to your energy. Those are the right people to be in your life. The ones who seek out and admire positivity and contentment.

The moment I truly became unbothered was when I realized that there was nothing anyone else could say or do that would change how I felt or reacted. I see it happening around me all the time. Some people who were able to control my moods and therefore actions by triggering me suddenly lost control. In the beginning, they were confused as to what was happening, and kept trying to go further and further to throw me off my game. I honestly feel sometimes it's not a deliberate action but a subconscious effort on their part. They are losing control over your life and that's not an easy pill to swallow, especially for people who are insecure and thrive on being able to control you to feed their own esteem.

Soon their little, almost harmless ploys turned into little criticisms about my new positive changes. I even had some of these people tell me I look worse after my health transformation. Well, guess what? Not for you to decide. I feel and look amazing! Truly unbothered. Then it changed into trying to do some sort of an "intervention" as if getting healthy and feeling good is some sort of a disorder that needs to be fixed! Then it changed into outbursts of attention seeking behavior, crying fits, or other passive aggressive ways to get back to me. The old me would certainly have caved way before this point, but for some reason the transformed me just doesn't care. Come to find out, you can love someone but still be you at the same time! Loving family members, friends, or even romantic partners does not mean changing yourself into how they need or want you to be. You can give love and still be you! Who knew?

The more I live for myself, the more I am capable of giving my love and attention to the select few I truly care about. It has been so much easier to give love and receive love when I was no longer owned by other people. The first step in freeing yourself from the control of others is to stop controlling or owning other people. Every single person in your life right now should be there by choice. Yes, even your children. We do not own them in any way. We give birth to them and love and nurture them into adulthood. That should be the extent of our relationship with them. Once they reach adulthood, we should hope to be friends with them in such a way that they truly want to be around us. They should never be obligated to do anything for us just because they happen to share our DNA. That's called blackmail. Stop blackmailing people into your life. Attract them into your life and invite them to stay with your love, grace, and friendship. Saying to the Universe that you are free while trying to control the actions of others is a huge contradiction. You are giving very conflicting instructions to the Universe and will never manifest your true desires with this approach. Set yourself free by letting others go free to live the life they desire.

Don't let the fear of losing people keep you from setting them free. You will be surprised to learn that allowing others to be who they are and coming from a place of acceptance will draw them into your life even more. Who doesn't want to feel loved, appreciated, and accepted for their true selves? The truth is when loved ones feel like they have to behave a certain way to gain our approval, it makes them very distant. They may try to be out of their natural comfort zone, but their inner true self will not allow them to put up with this act for very long. As a result, they will be exhausted in your presence since they are having to work extra hard to maintain the version you expect, instead of the person they truly are. Do you really want people to be exhausted in your presence? Or do you want them to feel loved, accepted, and rejuvenated in your company? Being true to myself, I greatly limit the amount of time I spend with people who don't accept me the way I am. It's mentally and physically exhausting for me not to be me!

During the liberation of others, you will for the first time feel free and liberated yourself. You will suddenly come to realize and notice the people in your own life that are holding you hostage. Even well-meaning family members can sometimes have that control over us. We have to re-train them to accept the true us. The first step in doing this is by showing them who we really are. This will certainly be a slow process, as they get to know us all over again, the real us, without any facades or expectations of conforming to their beliefs.

There are many people in my life whom I love and admire but don't necessarily share their belief systems. It's okay to not be a complete replica of someone else and still love and cherish them! You may even be surprised to find out that people will love and admire you more for truly being authentic and vulnerable. Sometimes it's our own fear of how they will perceive us that keeps us from showing our true selves.

During my real estate career, I had the pleasure of meeting a young Muslim man that ended up teaching me a very important lesson. He was a college student who was doing real estate on the side to pay his bills, just like myself, and I truly admired him. He was working on a deal with my mother and frequented our office. During one of his visits, he looked very sad so my mother probed him on what was wrong, even though he kept trying to convince her that he was fine. He finally broke down crying and told us he was gay and was very afraid of his family finding it out. He said earlier that day he had planned out his suicide in the event that his father found out about his lifestyle.

My heart broke for him and I couldn't hold back my tears. My son was one year old at the time and I decided at that point that I would have completely failed as a parent and human being if my child felt they couldn't come to me with something so important that they would rather kill themselves instead. Being a safe place for my husband and children is very important to me.

Knowing my mother to be a very emotional person, I expected that upon hearing this she would also be crying. "Shame on you!" She screamed at him instead. Shocked at her reaction and afraid of what she might say next, I literally came from behind my desk in case I needed to escort her out. "You are in the unique position of helping the many other boys in your situation by standing up to your beliefs. But instead, you are going to end your life without ever giving your parents a true chance of acceptance. What a waste of your life and your parents' love."

Over the several years we knew him, my mother slowly encouraged him to put his fear aside and give his parents a fair chance of showing their love and acceptance. I don't know if he was ever able to show the truest version of himself to his parents. The truth is there is no way to know how someone will react until they actually react. No matter how much we may know someone, we have to give them the chance instead of deciding in our heads on how they will react. Up until that one incident, I didn't even know where my mother stood on the topic. Even though we were best friends, it had simply never come up. What if he was basing his fear on the assumption that his parents would be upset? And even if they were upset, I'm pretty sure they would have not wanted him to commit suicide.

Every time I do more inner work and upgrade my identity, I give those around me a chance to update their mental and energetic database to get accustomed to the new me. They are allowed to have their own emotional reaction and experience and I am allowed to be me.

Expanded Edition Update:

I would say I am definitely more unbothered and unphased by others' opinions of me and my choices now. This has taken a lot of work and continues to compound in my life. The truth is that I owe it to my ancestors to make something amazing out of my life. This is the most access to rights, freedom, choices, and abundance that anyone in my ancestry has had. It is both my birthright and my duty to use my time here wisely. I want to honor my ancestors' journey while also laying down some solid roots and foundations for my descendants.

Knowing my place in my lineage has helped me stay in my own lane and not mess with any distractions on the way, no matter how shiny or enticing. I trust that everyone else is following their own soul blueprint and will figure it out.

If you don't have solid boundaries around your time and energy, the world will impose its own agendas and timelines on you. Most people have good intentions but bad focus, and it doesn't take much to let time slip away from us. Having children who I know are watching and learning from me has helped keep me on my best game.

Affirmation:

"I owe it to my ancestors to live my best life!"

JOURNAL PROMPTS FOR REFLECTION:

What do you need to stop believing to be really, truly unbothered?

_____

_____

_____

What assumptions do you make about others that keeps you from being unbothered?

_____

_____

_____

What is your process of letting people in your life know about your new identity and ways of being?

_____

_____

_____

CHAPTER
Eight
YOUR HUMANS

Always be a first-rate version of yourself, instead of a second-rate version of somebody else. – Judy Garland

O nce you have learned the art of purging your commitments and keeping the people and things around that serve your soul and bring you joy, life will start to become a lot easier and a whole lot more fun! It will be easy to pinpoint the relationships you want to nurture and grow. Once you have released people from your control and set yourself free in the process, relationships will become easier to maintain. Conversations and even silence will flow freely and naturally. There will be no daunting work, games, or strategies in getting your spouse to do this or that. Love and trust will slowly build and grow.

I have learned that when we are not giving love and attention to ourselves and feeling insecure as a result, we unnaturally fixate and attach ourselves to others. We are missing our own love and acceptance, so we leach onto others in hopes of receiving it from them. I'm sure you have heard the age-old adage that "the faster you chase something, the faster it runs away." Stop chasing, stop wanting, and needing, and start living by giving. Give to yourself first and foremost. Pay yourself first. Once you have established a healthy relationship with yourself and gained your own love, respect, and acceptance, only then you are in the position to give love and acceptance to others.

Once we release our loved ones of all the expectations and constraints we have put on them to fill the empty voids, you free them to love the way they need to love us. Those voids were never anyone else's responsibility to fill. The truth is they can't fill those voids even if they wanted to. We alone have the power to mend ourselves. In my own life, the more I loved, appreciated, and accepted myself, the less I needed my husband to love, appreciate, and accept me. The more I freed him from these responsibilities, the more he loved, appreciated, and accepted me. The truth is he had loved me all along. I just never saw it because I wanted him to tell me while he is the type of man that shows me instead. It wasn't until I learned to speak and understand his language of love that I finally understood him and felt connected on a more intimate level.

Just because someone doesn't love us in the exact manner that we are demanding, doesn't mean there isn't love. In all honesty, I would much rather have him show me his love in his many daily actions then repeatedly tell me he loves me but behave otherwise. When I freed him to be as he is, I not only started to see all of his love, but he started expressing it verbally the way I wanted him to. Funny how that works, isn't it?

The same goes for relationships with siblings, parents, and even in-laws. Once we have achieved control over our many insecurities, we come to see that not everything others say or do is an attack to our ego. Insecurity magnifies and intensifies even the most casual of encounters or disagreements with others. We are quick to make excuses for our own often unreasonable actions and behaviors, but when it comes to others, we are quick to call it malicious intent.

One powerful technique I have come to adapt when it comes to dealing with family members is to view them as friends. We have this belief that friends we choose and family we are stuck with and deal with. Your goal should be to achieve friendship and respect with your family members. If such can't be achieved then we can choose to be respectful without making them feel obligated to us in any way. There shouldn't be demands or expectations that our family members should do for us because we are family. Again, that's blackmail. You can't hold someone hostage just because you share their DNA or are tied to them through marriage.

Children are undoubtedly the most abused group in this regard than any other. Because they are dependent on us to meet even their most basic needs, we come to exert ownership and power over them. The only right we have is to love, nurture, and mentor them through life. It is not for us to decide what they choose to do with themselves or control them into becoming idealized versions of ourselves. They are not required to share your dreams or ambitions. They are born with their own set of passions and desires and have every right to fulfill them. Treat them as little humans with a fully developed soul instead of little, unknowing children that you need to mold into perfect adults.

I have come to believe that children who see their parents as individual people with their own set of shortcomings, abilities, passions, and desires instead of simply "my parents" have the ability to do this with their children as well. When you ask a 3-year-old what their mommy's name is, they reply "mommy." I think most of us never outgrow that ability to see our parents in light of anything except as our parents. Since they were and will always be a person and being, simply filling a role as a parent, they will always disappoint us if we never see beyond this one role.

If you are lucky enough to be blessed with your parents still in your life, make the transition today. Allow them to be a fully autonomous, and sovereign person that they were created to be and release them from the confinements of being your mother or father. Understand that they are humans just like you and forgive them for all the mistakes they have made. Even if you have a strained relationship with a parent and have chosen not to be a part of their life, forgive them. Forgiveness does not mean you have to allow them access to you, but it does mean letting go of resentments and freeing up that emotional energy for other creative pursuits.

It is only after you have made this transition in thought that you can in turn see your children as individual entities. This in turn will start the cycle of your own children accepting you as a person with faults, passions, and desires who happens to be their parent. Someone in this position is allowed to make mistakes, grow, learn, evolve, and still be capable of love, respect, acceptance, and friendship.

Encourage independent thought and the room to make mistakes when your children look to you for guidance. I have very strong, opinionated stances on a lot of things, but when speaking with my children I make it clear that it's important for them to form their own opinions on things. I encourage this by saying "This is how I feel based on what I have learnt and my lived experiences, what are your thoughts?" I always tell them that their thoughts and feelings will change as they grow, experience, and learn new things, and to keep revisiting and updating their stances on the various areas of life. They are lifelong learners of their own destiny. Let them know that you will love them no matter what path they choose. Even if you don't always agree with their decisions, you will love them. They won't always agree with you either, and that's okay. Love is not contingent on beliefs or the individual paths they take in the quest towards happiness. And do everyone a favor and stop saying "I'm happy as long as you're happy," just to turn around and convince yourself that they are not happy and you should intervene. Not your place, learn to mind your own business. And yes, tell them you love and accept them, even if you think they know this, talk to them.

Deciding how or what makes someone truly happy is an impossible task. You never know if your family member is just going along with what you like in order to gain your approval or if it truly is the real them. I see this happening all around me and from the thousands of women writing in to me through my You-Tube channel. When a couple gets married, the guy or girl's family believes they truly know the real them and the new spouse is the outsider. Anything new or different the couple does that is outside the realm of their family beliefs is always faulted on the spouse. I have often made this mistake myself. When my own siblings were married or in relationships, I would chalk any new behavior as being the influence of this new person. Convincing myself that my sibling must be so unhappy for having been forced upon this change. Every time this has happened, I have come to find out that it was my sibling in fact that made that switch in the comfort and acceptance of their newfound freedom. I was in fact pigeon holing them into a certain role because they had acted it out to please me!

This is true especially in cultures where family members are expected to behave in certain ways without much clear communication. There is love and respect, but without clear communication people aim to please without revealing their own trueness. In smaller doses this is easy to maintain. Once you are married and living with someone permanently, your true natures, needs, desires, and wants quickly become evident. Any changed behavior on your part is mistaken as your spouse controlling and changing your behavior. You instantly go into "my poor son/daughter/brother/sister is being controlled. Look he/she no longer does this or is doing this now. He/she must not be happy." Sound familiar? Stop it. You never know what goes on behind closed doors in the sanctuary of marriage and love. Stop inserting yourself into other people's lives and dig deeper within your own inner soul. Ask yourself, how may I serve myself today?

Expanded Edition Update:

I am definitely clearer on what kind of role model I want to be for those that matter deeply to me. I have learned that the best way to teach is through our own embodiment. My mother used to give me the best advice, but I never really valued it because she wasn't embodied in it. To my children I give the gift of embodiment and role modeling, knowing that they have their own unique soul blueprint.

Today I am blessed with 3 wonderful children that not only value my guidance and opinions on all things but also thank me for giving them a blueprint for life. I never try to enforce my beliefs or opinions on them but remain available to have deep conversations on any and all topics that interest them. They are naturally very curious about life and we encourage them to form their own personal values through curiosity and being a student of life. Having a growth mindset is very important to my family.

Having Armaan grow into a "young adult" has been a huge learning curve for us as parents. Transitioning to letting Armaan make his own decisions even if we don't agree with them has taken us some inner work and expanded our own beliefs on parenting. We allow him to be his own person and young man while also letting him know of our experienced opinion and then allow him to choose for himself. We are available for emotional support and guidance but let him take ownership of his decisions through natural consequences as much as possible.

Affirmations:

"My worthiness is never in question."

"I am fully capable of figuring it out."

JOURNAL PROMPTS
FOR REFLECTION:

What parts of yourself are you still hiding and from whom? What do you fear would happen if you finally shared that part of you? Is that really true or a story that you have made up in your mind?

_____

_____

_____

How can you allow others to be more authentic in your presence? How would being more authentic change the relationship dynamic between you and your loved ones?

_____

_____

_____

CHAPTER
Nine
THE MOST BEAUTIFUL WOMAN IN THE ROOM

There is no cosmetic for beauty like happiness.
– Lady Blessington

Learning the art of self-care is an important aspect of our journey towards self-love of both inner and outer beauty. Fertilize and nurture your soul by spending time and focus on both your inner being and outer shell. You do this by respecting your time, energy, and focus in life. By nurturing your body with good, real, whole food, exercising for health, spending time with people that matter and doing only the things that bring you joy. Now that you have learned not only to purge distractions but also to manage your time efficiently, it's time to shift your attention on what you could be doing with some of your time. Self-care to me means taking the time to pay myself some extra love and attention. I do this by reading, learning, and making sure to invest in my growth. This is important to me so I spend some time accomplishing this every single day. This is my biggest gift to myself. Another way I nurture myself is to take care of my outer shell, my body, by showing it love through proper personal grooming. Grooming is an important part of my wellbeing, one I take great pride and joy in. It shows the world that I take pride in ownership over every aspect of my life and wellbeing while also pleasing our internal audience. Not everyone will understand or enjoy this, and that is exactly why you need to take the time to learn what brings you joy and satisfaction. When I take the time to care for my hair, skin, and nails, as well as my inner passion for learning and growing, I truly feed my soul and feel at home in my body.

I believe that your hair, skin, and nails are windows into the inner state of your overall health and wellness. If your nutrition, sleep, or stress levels are off balance, these are often the first places to show signs of wear and tear, and sometimes quite literally. If my hair, skin, and nails are being affected on the outside, I can't even imagine what might be happening to my insides. If your nutrition, fitness, and stress levels are in fact on point, yet you are not seeing the results you would like, it's time to reevaluate the damage or neglect you might be subjecting these areas to. Remember we only have one body. Our younger selves can do a lot of damage, and for the time being can get away with it. It eventually catches up to us, and there may be no turning back the clock at that point. So, take care of what you have, and don't let it go without putting up a fight.

The best piece of advice I ever read was to treat your hair like a fine piece of silk garment. Wash, dry, and style it with gentle care. I haven't always had the healthiest hair and thought it was in my genes to be balding by my mid-30's like many of my other female relatives. Come to find out, I can control my hair destiny by changing my lifestyle habits. Over the years through healthy eating, restful sleep, and managing my stress, I have finally achieved my dream of having long, healthy, luscious locks. I take care of it with pride and wear it with joy. I make sure to get a strong dose of micronutrients and vitamins from real, whole foods. It really all begins with good nutrition. I don't wash my hair daily, use gentle shampoos when I do, and condition it with oils to keep it strong and healthy. I use the gentlest dryer setting when drying it and braid it loosely before bed every night to protect it from wear and tear while I sleep. I color my grays with only good quality professional hair color and give myself weekly oil treatments. And I tell the Universe every single day how appreciative I am for my healthy hair.

I have been blessed with good skin for most of my life, and great nutrition and lifestyle habits have only enhanced it further. Remember to always eat, sleep, and exercise for beauty. There isn't any one special potion that will cure all your skincare woes. Nourish your body from the inside out, and you will truly glow from within. Make sure to get all your micronutrients through eating a rainbow of fruits and vegetables.

Consider any skincare issues that arise as your internal body's call for help. Anytime my skin acts up and I get a pimple, my first thought is to examine my diet and stress levels for the previous few days. The way I look at it, my skin isn't craving the newest skincare fad, it's acting up because it needs me to make a behavioral change. My body knows that a pimple will quickly get my attention, and I will examine and modify my last few days' worth of abuse. So, instead of adding a new skincare product in, see what you can remove from your life to relieve your skin's burden.

If you are after that lit from within radiance, the only formula I know for that besides nutrition, sleep, exercise, and stress management is to light up your soul. This can be achieved by following the steps in this book and finding and living your true passions. Let the little things slide off your back. Don't sweat the small stuff and truly focus attention on yourself and your passions. Feeding your inner soul will light it up with an angelic glow that no skincare product can ever come close to achieving. No one else can do this for you, so really, it's time to stop blaming others for our own neglect and abuse.

Now don't get me wrong, I am a girly girl at heart and love my skincare and makeup, but I always aim to work from the inside out. My skin is my canvas. I dare not apply makeup on a dirty canvas. Aim to fix the underlying issues as well as putting on skincare and makeup. Layering concealer and foundation over skin that is begging for your attention is like applying perfume when you really need a shower. May work in the short time, but who are you really fooling? Take the time and care to figure out what is causing problems in your skin. Is it your diet, stress, lifestyle, or hormones? Well, all of these things can be fixed, but only you can fix them. As for my personal skin rules to live by, I never ever sleep in my makeup. I make sure I wash my face thoroughly every single night. I have been wearing makeup for over 15 years and have yet to miss washing my face at night. If you often forget or are too tired to wash off your makeup at night, then keep a pack of makeup removing wipes on your bedside table. Not a complete substitute for washing your face but much better than sleeping in your makeup.

Another tip is to aim for quality over quantity when it comes to makeup and skincare. When I first started my YouTube channel over 5 years ago, I was shocked to see the number of skincare and makeup items girls used every single day! I have been using a fourth of the products. I started thinking maybe it was better to use more, which led me into buying a lot more products than ever before. YouTube can certainly have that effect on you. It quickly became evident that the more makeup products I used, the more skincare items I needed to fix my suddenly arising skin issues. It didn't take me long to go back to my way of being a minimalist in both my beauty and skincare routine. So carefully examine your current beauty ritual and see what items you can remove. Even if you feel the need for more makeup and skincare right now, remember when you overhaul your diet, fitness, and overall health, you will have naturally radiant and glowing skin. You can slowly switch to a very basic makeup routine that only enhances your natural beauty, not covers it up.

I have always had a very simple and basic makeup routine. In that brief moment when I let YouTube influence my judgment, I remember going to my son's school or athletic events and people would stare at me. I was walking around with a really full face of make-up and lashes galore, probably looking like a clown. One of the benefits of being able to go back and see myself in my videos is to see what works and what doesn't. Covering up my natural skin and features with layers of makeup was doing nothing for my beauty. I quickly switched back to my original routine of wearing makeup to enhance my look, not mask it up. I understand that makeup is a huge fashion statement and lots of girls use it to express their creativity. If that's you, that's awesome! Just make sure you thoroughly clean your face at night and apply a good moisturizer. It's definitely important to stay true to what you love and enjoy.

When it comes to your nails, the same rule of health applies as hair and skin. Your nails will reflect the state of your internal affairs. You can slap on nail polish or treat yourself to the nicest manicures and pedicures, but they won't be healthy until you change your diet. Now that my nails aren't always brittle and breaking off, I no longer find myself wanting to go to the salon. I alternate between painting my nails to just putting on a clear top coat. You don't have to keep your nails painted to achieve a nice, clean, put together look. Pay some attention to trimming and filing your nails and add a shiny topcoat if you desire.

This small attention to details is what differentiates women who look well-tended and cared for from those who don't. You might think no one is noticing, but remember the VIP we are trying to impress is ourselves, through our internal audience! The small efforts that you make in your personal grooming will bring you back miles of confidence. Every single thing, however small, that we do for ourselves feeds our self-esteem. It makes us confident and take pride in our overall well being and look. Ever wonder what makes some women appear rich and look expensive in the most basic of attire, while others are decked out in expensive clothes and designer accessories, yet don't appear put together? The difference can always be chalked up to overall appearance of health and attention to detail to their grooming. Any woman can go buy nice clothes and accessories, but that will never be a substitute for care and attention, especially if you want to exude radiance. So, if you truly want to stand out, take the extra steps and truly invest in your overall health. A woman who is healthy, fit, and radiant will always catch more attention than the one who is simply decked out in the latest designer wear.

Over the years, I have slowly learned how to take care of all my grooming needs myself. I bought a basic waxing kit from Amazon and learned how to wax. It only took me a couple of tries to learn it to perfection. With thousands of YouTube tutorials on any topic, anything is possible! I used to pay $150 every

3 weeks for these services. Not to mention the time wasted commuting back and forth and long waiting times at the salons. My second money and time saving switch came when I started touching up my own roots in between hair appointments. I have been plagued with graying hair since I was 16 years old, so I have to color my roots quite often. I was paying around $40-$200 at the hair salon every month depending on what else I was talked into doing while I was there. Not to mention all that time wasted. If you can't tell by now, I am that rare woman that actually does not enjoy sitting around in salons. I don't find it relaxing at all, and usually can't wait to get out of there. Now my stylist comes to my house to trim and color my hair every 3-4 months, and in between appointments I touch up my own roots. Saves so much in time and money. Using these tips have helped me especially in this season of life when my children are young. Remember that as we live through our various seasons of life, we get to update our needs and desires accordingly.

I have been a work from home/stay at home mom for more than 7 years now. Despite this I always take the time to get dressed and look presentable every day. You know the old saying of "dressing for the job you want and not the job you have," well it's true! My 5-year-old son dresses like a superhero on most evenings because he wants to be a superhero when he grows up. So, take a cue from him and start dressing like the goddess that you are destined to become. Now I'm not saying be uncomfortable. There is a happy marriage between comfort and looking gorgeous at the same time. Also remember that what we are "comfortable" with changes as we grow. I am very un-comfortable wearing sweats because that is not who I am. I don't even own any sweats, but for others that is their comfort zone and they go everywhere in sweats. Who's looking, you say? You are! I dress to impress myself. No matter what anyone else says or thinks about my clothes or makeup, the truth is if I feel good in what I'm wearing, I can conquer the world. In fact, any time I have tried to dress to impress other peo-ple, I have been the most uncomfortable person in the room, even in the fanciest of outfits. I dress to impress myself and that makes me feel like the happiest, most beautiful, and most confident woman in any room.

My number one suggestion to being able to effort-lessly get dressed is to find a signature style. What out-fits do you currently own that put that extra bounce in your step? If you could only choose to wear one outfit for the rest of your life, what would it be? If you sud-denly had to leave all your clothes behind, what would you choose to take with you? Use that as a template to create future outfits. I'm a huge believer and follower of the KonMari Method. Read her book and imple-ment her method to find the items that truly bring you joy. Then learn to buy only those items. Remember more clothes are not always better. I am now left with less than 100 total items of clothing, but they all fit my style, body, complement my skin tone, and bring me utter joy to wear. This has made getting dressed so much more fun and easier in the mornings. I also don't constantly have the need to shop. A feeling that stems from having too many things that don't flatter us or fit our current body size. When I have a ton of clothes in my closet crowding my judgment, I feel like I have nothing to wear, and it makes me want to shop impulsively. Now that I only have items that I love and fit, I shop with much more intention. Find those pieces and then stop saving them for special occasions. How amazing would it be to wear what you love every single day! This is only possible when every single item you own brings you joy.

Once you figure out your style, make your selections in colors that truly complement your skin tone, eye, and hair color. What are some colors that you love to wear? What colors get you the most compliments from others? Better yet have your colors professionally done. Sometimes people will compliment a color we are wearing not because we look good in it, but the color itself is competing with our skin tone and winning! Ouch! It's okay to own multiples in colors that really suit you. I have always enjoyed wearing blues and greens. I used to feel guilty for owning multiple items in those colors and would force myself to buy other colors but then never wear them. What a waste! Buy things that bring you joy and make you feel good, and get rid of all the distractions. This can be tough in the beginning. When I did a huge overhaul using KonMari's methods, it was a shock for the first week or so to see my almost bare closet. I realized quickly how much easier it was to get dressed despite having so many fewer items of clothing. Everything I now own fits and looks amazing on me. It puts decision making in the morning on autopilot. And no matter what outfit I choose to wear, I know it flatters my style and my body.

One thing to keep in mind is not to get caught up in other people's ideas of having a certain number of pieces or certain color palettes to be able to mix and match. Aim for the number that naturally comes to be after you only keep and buy items that bring you joy. I personally tend to shop impulsively when I keep buying the wrong things and have a closet full of the wrong items. When everything I own brings me joy and fits my style, I shop more intentionally. A lot of the mix and match and x number of capsule wardrobes focus on a cookie cutter approach. Many of the ones I saw lack the colors and designs that bring me joy. So obviously they are not for me. I don't worry about my items working with each other. My style is pretty predictable and hasn't changed much in the last 15 years, only taking a slight detour and pause during my pregnancies and postpartum days. As soon as I got my body back, I naturally reverted back to my signature style. Jeans or black pants with a cute, flowy, attention-grabbing top. My absolutely favorite tops have cold shoulders and bell sleeve tops. That's what I wore for most of my 20s and continue to enjoy wearing into my mid-30s. Any time I have been inspired to change that style based on someone else's idea of "classic," I have regretted it and reverted back to my own signature style.

When it comes to accessories, I like to invest a little more money into these items. Sunglasses, shoes, and handbags is where I invest the bulk of my wardrobe money. I have learned to buy them in neutral colors so they don't compete with the bright tops that I wear. Any time I have bought bright colored accessories, it's been much harder to match with my bright color palette of clothing. Since I spent a little more money on my accessories, they last longer, and I can have less without the need to constantly update them. When I do fall out of love with an item, I sell it and use that money to buy a more updated version that I love. I have slowly stopped wearing cosmetic jewelry. Just didn't work with my overall look and again always competed with my bright color tops. Instead, I choose to invest in a few pieces of fine jewelry and wear those same pieces every single day. Eliminates clutter both in my closet and appearance and I find this to be a more elegant look for myself.

Expanded Edition Update:

I have since had my colors done professionally and it has been a game changer! I learned that many of the colors I received the most compliments on were not the right color for me. Notice if people compliment your beauty or the color itself. If they compliment the color, that's usually not the best sign. It means the color is probably washing you out and standing out against your beauty. I now purchase mostly the colors that make me look my most vibrant and radiant!

A few years ago, I also discovered the Kibbe system for body types on YouTube. It was so interesting to learn what types of outfits work the best for my body shape and how the flesh sits on my bones to create the masculine and feminine aspects of my body and overall look. I highly recommend this system for anyone that is interested. David Kibbe has an out-of-print book that I was able to purchase on eBay, however most of the information can be found online in groups, forums, and YouTube videos. I believe he is writing a new book at the moment.

One major change for me is that I have completely stopped wearing pants. It was funny to read this chapter and remember how I used to only wear pants. I spent most of my previous life believing I had ugly legs! Once I got over this and activated full acceptance and self-love for my body, I started trying on dresses and skirts. I instantly started to feel so feminine and free, and I swear people treat me so much better now! Nothing against pants, but I only prefer dresses and skirts now. It makes me feel way more feminine and freer.

I still get dressed daily and prefer to do most of my beauty stuff at home as much as possible. Yes, I'm still very much a homebody and introverted, that part hasn't changed. I do get my hair done professionally once a month. My nails and lashes twice a month usually. I get massages a couple times a month and that's about it. I have not gotten into Botox, fillers, facials or anything else at this point in my life. Nothing against any of these things, but I don't feel the need for them at this point.

The biggest part of my self-care has been my inner work. Wow, what a difference that has made in my life! Journaling, meditation, and walking in nature are some of my favorite self-care activities. Inner work has helped me gain self-awareness and emotional control. It's been the reason I now have a thriving, happy, calm, abundant life. I was on a call yesterday, and my client asked me if I had any dirty laundry in my life? Not really. If dirty laundry shows up, we simply wash it up! I like to clean up the areas of my life that need attention, and keep evolving and growing! Ignoring or letting things fester takes up too much emotional energy.

From an evolutionary perspective, women like to know that we are the "most" in something. Most beautiful, most kind, most feminine. This does not mean we are competing with others; we just want to be seen, heard, and appreciated for something that is uniquely ours. My entire perception of myself changed when I started saying the following affirmation: *"I am the most beautiful woman in every room."* I have no idea if I suddenly became the most beautiful woman or just started feeling like it, but honestly, I don't care! I always feel like I AM the most beautiful woman in every room, and that's the most important thing. Everyone else also seems to treat me like I am, and I love it!

Affirmation:

"I am the most beautiful woman in every room."

JOURNAL PROMPTS
FOR REFLECTION:

What do I need to upgrade about my self-care that would make me feel like the most beautiful woman in every room?

_____

_____

_____

What area of my body is screaming out for my attention? How can I show it more love?

_____

_____

_____

What are my go to outfit combinations? Am I happy with this? How can I use this as a template to create future outfits effortlessly?

_____

_____

_____

CHAPTER
Ten
PUT YOUR MONEY WHERE YOUR SOUL IS

Don't let making a living prevent you from making a life.
-John Wooden

There is a reason why this chapter ended up at the end of my book and not in the beginning. It's certainly not because I think wealth isn't a big part of life. But that's just it, it's just one part of life, yet many people give it their biggest focus and attention. Focusing on only one area of your life while neglecting all others will quickly throw your life off balance. In my own life and many of those I have been around and worked with, money seems to crawl in one door and quickly fly out the other. Then we try to fill the void that can only be mended with nurturing our bodies and souls by buying things. Lots and lots of things. It's really a nev-er-ending cycle and trust me I have also been caught in that trap. My heart was in the right place, but my wallet was always in the wrong place. For this reason, even with the ability to attract money easily and quickly into my life, I was never really good at keeping money.

Now if you have been following my journey on YouTube, then you already know that clutter and the accumulation of things gives me anxiety. I can't think clearly when I am surrounded by things, especially things I am not using. I definitely get this from my father, who had a full-blown anxiety disorder his whole life, we just didn't know there was a name for his of-ten-strange behavior. As he got older, his disorder grew to a point of no return. He doesn't leave his room, talk to people, and is probably the most pessimistic person I know. Due to this I have always been cautious of fixing my anxiety before it completely overtook my life. He also had a huge aversion to clutter, there would be days where he would frantically throw things out, even useful things, in trying to reclaim his environment.

When I was living on my own with just my son, I kept my condo pretty streamlined and the number of overall items to a safe number I could deal with. Since I was also constantly shopping, this meant I was always giving away bags and bags of things, sometimes never used or only slightly used, to friends and fami-ly. In my lifetime, I have probably given away tenfold of the number of things I have actually used and en-joyed. What a complete waste. It makes me sad to look back and think how much that money would have been worth had I invested it instead. I chose instead to spend it on things that didn't bring me any joy and have since been long forgotten.

It wasn't until I met my husband that I was forced to finally confront my bad relationship with money. Somewhere along the lines of living to meet the demands of life instead of living with intent, I had lost myself. Unknowingly, I was trying to feed that insecurity through the constant accumulation of things. Since having lots of things was not in line with my inner soul and personal values, I was also always purging those items onto others, stuck in a never-ending vicious cycle. I believe when we do things that are not in line with our true nature, our entire being resists it. Too busy with life, I never had the chance to take a moment to ask myself some very important questions.

In the beginning, I strongly resisted my husband's money habits. I figured there was something wrong with him, and worried that he had the inability to enjoy money. I spent the first year or two of marriage thinking he was trying to control me. When in fact he had been sent to me by the Universe to force me to look in the mirror and focus on healing myself. As I got to know him further, I started admiring his contentment with the things he had without the constant need to be buying stuff. Not to say that he didn't learn from me either, in all honesty I have probably helped him to live a little and learn to enjoy his money a bit more. There is definitely a happy medium that we have achieved over the years. Even though I slowly started realizing that his relationship with money was a lot healthier than mine and slowly started adapting his way; I never truly felt in sync with him when it came to finances. Even though I followed along and wanted my children to learn his behavior over mine, I wasn't emotionally and spiritually where I needed to be. Through the gradual process of discovering my true desires and values and working to heal every single aspect of my health and wellbeing, I slowly started towards a new relationship with money.

It started with me buying and shopping a lot less and giving every purchase more thought. Would I really use this? Would it bring me happiness? Would I just give it away? YouTube was a bad influence on me during this transition. I had made some online friends, mostly other YouTubers, who were constantly shopping and doing hauls. Would I lose subscribers if I suddenly stopped shopping and doing hauls, I worried? I mentioned I was transitioning my channel slowly into what I had truly intended for it in the first place, a safe place for women to come and feel positive and inspired. Some of these friends started speaking to me a lot less and less until there was nothing left for us to talk about. I guess shopping was the only thing that connected us. This made me worry more about the connection I would lose with my subscribers if I shifted the focus of my channel.

I started reading finance blogs which lead to Thomas J. Stanley and his research on how the average millionaire lives in the US. I was intrigued with his books, The Millionaire Next Door[15] and Millionaire Mind.[16] I was finally starting to understand how and why my husband was the way he was. He very well understood that you don't get rich by spending money, you get rich by saving and investing it. I loved how the millionaires in Stanley's books had achieved their wealth from living a comfortable, mindful, and content lifestyle. Armed with the passion to achieve this money mindfulness, I vowed this to be a major step in my personal growth and development.

I took a long break from YouTube to further focus on my fitness and ponder and think about the future direction of my channel without being influenced by outside forces. I needed to be certain that the final decision came from a place inside of me. I came back refreshed and slowly transitioned my channel away from shopping and into more positive and inspiring videos. The response I got was overwhelmingly positive. It was like I had finally found my niche, something I was made to do. I did lose a lot of subscribers, but the ones I gained and the ones who stayed were the right match for me. These people weren't my friends because I simply had the right handbag or accessories, they were there to connect with me, the whole and real me.

During this time, I redid my vision board for the New Year and asked the Universe for more growth and clarity of mind among my usual list of things that rarely change from year after year. I asked for true financial security, not the one that comes from having money, but the one that comes with feeling contentment and complete financial freedom.

During this time, I discovered Marie Kondo, and it was like a lightbulb went on. I needed to make that joy and money connection to truly have my money serve me in a way that felt good. I quickly introduced my husband to the method. He was also intrigued. Although my husband is good with saving money, he has trouble letting go of things. It doesn't necessarily stem from an emotional place, but savers often see dollar signs being thrown away with the trash. We spent an entire month cleaning out every corner of the house. He had things collected over decades, CDs, DVDs, and hundreds of knick-knacks.

The more we got rid of, the lighter, freer, and more at home we felt. It suddenly started making sense to me why I never felt at home in South Carolina. I had walked into a whole bunch of his stuff, collected over years and years, things I had no connection with or control over. I was literally feeling suffocated but could not do anything to take control of my surroundings. I felt a little better when we moved to Texas and I was able to put a lot of that stuff out of sight at least, but I knew it was all there, sitting around collecting dust and making me very uncomfortable.

Don't get me wrong, I'm not some sort of a control freak that wants to completely erase my husband's previous life from our home. I just don't do well with collections of things that serve no purpose and get no use. But since these were not my things to give away, I felt out of control in my own home. Through this process of editing our entire home and a huge overhaul of mindset, I felt connected to my husband in a very different way that I cannot even express in words. Together, we have vowed to be very selective and conscious of every item that makes its way into our home. If it doesn't serve a purpose and bring us utter joy, it's not coming in the door.

We work way too hard in our lives to spend our money, time, and energy surrounded by things that don't serve us. This liberation from the control of things makes my soul feel so light and airy, I honestly feel like I can fly. Knowing that I have the option to buy anything and everything my heart desires but choosing not to, is true financial security and independence in my eyes. Things no longer own me, and shopping is no longer an unintentional coping mechanism. I not only attract money easily into my life, but once it's here, it stays, and grows.

Suddenly my fear of losing my beloved subscribers has turned into a mission of sharing my transformation. I am not done yet, I will continue to learn and grow, and I encourage you to do the same. Please take the time to ask yourself the important questions. Find your mission statement, your end goal, and your legacy. Rearrange your life to focus on those goals and get rid of all the distractions. Eat for beauty, health, and vitality. Spend time on self-care, nurturing both your soul and your beautiful body. Gain the confidence to say no to other people's ideas of how you should live your life, and through this process become unbreakable. Reevaluate where you spend your money and the people and things you allow into your sacred space. That includes your mind, heart, and home.

Expanded Edition Update:

So, I was right about not being done with inner work yet!! Great call, 2016 Mina! So much has changed and evolved in the money department for us!!

We have since learned that money has both feminine and masculine aspects of it, and as with creating anything in life, you need both to manifest it. The feminine aspects of money have to do with your beliefs and relationships around it. This impacts your ability to attract it and with how much ease. The masculine aspects of money have to do with your ability to create structures around it by allocating it to your desires, needs, wants, and also investing for your future self.

When hubby and I got married, he had the masculine part down and needed work in the feminine aspects of money. He could earn it through his job and save it, but only in an expected linear fashion. He also lacked the ability to manifest more and truly enjoy what he had. I, on the other hand, could manifest money all day long, but it never stayed for long. I lacked the ability to create structure and legacy around my money. We have since learned from each and have fixed our individual relationship with money, which has in turn changed our legacy together.

We are now financially independent and free. Meaning neither one of us needs to work for another penny ever again. We both choose to pursue our passions which bring in money in addition to our portfolio. However, we don't need to work. Interestingly enough, once we stopped needing to work for money, money started raining on us. Passion and service is such a huge activator of money as long as we have fixed our relationship with money.

I now own and run an eight-figure company from the comfort of my dream home in my spare time, when I feel like it. Could life really be this magical, yes, only when we allow it! I will share a bit more about my life in the new expanded chapter of this book!

Affirmations:

"I get paid to exist."

"I make money effortlessly and easily."

"Money loves me and flows to me with ease and grace."

JOURNAL PROMPTS FOR REFLECTION:

What is my current relationship with money? Am I able to attract it with ease and flow? Do I have healthy structures around it to spend, enjoy, and invest in ways aligned with my values?

_____

_____

_____

Do I need more work in feminine aspects of money or masculine aspects of money?

_____

_____

_____

CHAPTER
Eleven
INTERSECTION OF IDENTITIES

Some people live the same year 80 times and call it a lifetime.
Others collapse many lifetimes into one human life experience. -
Mina Irfan

Hi, this is the 2023 Incarnation of Mina Irfan. Sitting here reading and expanding on this book in August of 2023 has been such a surreal experience. The first edition of this book was published in 2016. Reading back, it's clear to me now that I was at the intersection of two identities. My Self-Aware Barbie™ era was ending and the Million Dollar Babe™ era was beginning.

Having this book to look back on is such a true testament of my inner work and everything I currently teach, including my 4 stages of consciousness. Before

I get into those with you, let me give you a current update of my life.

I am now a 42 year old feminine woman living the life of my wildest dreams. Actually, I don't think I could have even dreamed of the life that I live now. My relationship with my husband of 15 years, Irfan, has only gotten juicier, sexier, and more robust. We are best friends, lovers, partners, co-parents, and each other's greatest cheerleaders. Our union provides our 3 children a robust foundation and model of what a healthy relationship looks like. Our oldest son, Armaan is now almost 19, can you freaking believe it? We had some rough patches with him as he had to embark on his own healing journey. Mostly as a result of being born into a broken home and having been robbed of maternal and paternal presence in his earliest, most formative years. He is now a successful young man, finishing college while running his own business. He routinely thanks both Irfan and I for giving him a stable example of success in all areas of life, including healthy relationships. My son Ayaan is now 13 and Alina is now 9 years old! They are both happy, calm, well-balanced children who love spending time in nature.

When I wrote this book, I had a small life-coaching business generating six figures a year. In November of 2017, I ended up launching my first digital course and it was an instant success!! My students not only loved it but they wanted more!! I couldn't believe how effortless and easy it was for me to create online courses. Through this journey, I started activating my voice more and sharing more experiences and lessons from my culture and my education. My students love my unique marriage of science, spirituality, and culture that I share and teach. I now have over 60 digital courses, have done about 2 dozen in person events, and generated over eight figures from my company while helping tens of thousands of women from all over the world!

In 2022, hubby and I purchased an 8600 square foot mansion that was custom designed by an ex-NBA player! It's like he took the blueprint right out of my dreams and built this house. What's really eerie is that this house was built in 2005, which was one of the darkest, most rock bottom years of my life. To know that God had bigger and better plans for me at that time of my life makes me feel so loved and blessed.

That same year I also became the #1 seller for Thinkific, the platform I use to host all my courses, I held the top #2 position prior to that. I also had my first 7-figure month that year and learned that I am in the top 1% within the top 1% of earners in the United States. I have not only broken the glass ceiling, which never really existed in my mind, but have also raised the floor for future generations. I believe this and more is possible and available for all women and have continuously proven it with my clients and students.

Life is pure magic and I clearly see how I was unknowingly creating space in my life for these blessings and manifestations through all the mindsets and changes I wrote about in this book. The stuff I shared in this book may seem really simple, but it really works! In 2019, I downloaded, during a meditation, my 4 stages of consciousness. I immediately added it to my body of work and it has been a very helpful guide for me and my students to gauge and track our process.

Here is a brief description of the four stages. You can learn more about these stages as well as the male versions of them in my book, Lady Balls: How to Become Savagely Successful in a World Addicted to Suffering.

Please note that these stages may occur as percentages rather than definite states in most people. You may be 30% in one stage and 70% in another.

Basic Babe

The wounded inner child stage. In this stage, one sees themselves as powerless and as victims to people, places, and circumstances. Entitlement can also be a huge issue in this stage. They can be very childish in their mental processing and reasoning especially when triggered.

People in this stage are dependent on others to get their basic physical and emotional needs met. From their point of view, someone else is held responsible for their survival and wellbeing. That someone could be parents, siblings, romantic partners, friends or the government.

The Basic Babe is the forever damsel in distress and massive victim-hood. Everything is happening to the Basic Babe. She has no sense of responsibility and has given away her personal power to people, places, and circumstances. She is addicted to drama, complaining, and has low self-worth. She is often not receptive to love due to constricted heart center and low self-worth. Often addicted to drama, food, or gossip. Hoping to find a man to take care of them so they can go from mommy and daddy to someone else providing. A lot of their energy is used up in finding and keeping a man or drama with friends.

You are a Basic Babe, if you...

- Have trouble creating plans, structures, goals, and sticking to them.

- Have trouble making money and mostly rely on other people for manifesting things or money in your life.

- Are easily triggered and often lose control of your senses and emotions when in a triggered state.

- Feel like everyone is out to get you. It's always someone else's fault why you are not happy and successful in life.

- It always feels like you need someone else's permission before making even the simplest decisions in your life.

- Feel very dependent on others to get your basic emotional, physical, and financial needs met.

- Lack a sense of direction and purpose in your life.

If you relate to this, start your inner work immediately. I recommend finding a great therapist either in your area or online. You will need to do some inner child work and heal your mother and father wounds before advancing to the next stage. This will help activate your personal power and healthy masculine energy in your life. I have personally used Betterhelp for my therapy needs and loved the option of working with my therapist online. You can even change your therapist as many times as you need until you find the perfect match. Imagine my surprise when they reached out and wanted to offer my students a 10% discount off the first month of membership. You can use this link to activate your 10% discount:

https://betterhelp.com/TheUniverseGuru

How it works:

1. Sign up with Betterhelp using my affiliate link and get 10% off the already very LOW monthly fee.

    https://betterhelp.com/TheUniverseGuru

2. Choose your preferences for a therapist and wait for them to match you up with someone (it's super fast, I promise!). I got matched and was on a call with a therapist in less than 24 hours!

3. Start your healing journey!

FTC Disclaimer: I am proud to be sponsored by BetterHelp and they have given us a special link to get 10% off the first month of Online Therapy Services for my subscribers. I have used this company personally and would use them again in a heartbeat.

Self-Aware Barbie

This stage is activated when a woman's fight/flight response is turned on through life trauma or conditioning, putting the woman in her wounded masculine. This doesn't have to be something big, like childhood sexual abuse, like in my case. It could be as simple as growing up with a super masculine mother in a masculine society where achievements and structures are celebrated more than intuition and play. The Self-Aware Barbie takes personal responsibility for her triggers. In fact, she may overly blame herself even when it's not her fault! She catches her triggers and is actively working to rewire her neural pathways. She is taking back her personal power via hard work and determination. She is a go–getter, please-pleaser and chronic over giver. Usually has an over-developed masculine side. SABs are great at creating structures and disciplines for themselves and others.

An important thing to consider about SABs is that they activate the "predator" response in even generally good people. The truth is that most people are somewhere in the middle of the human animal vs conscious divine being spectrum. They are generally good but may choose to act questionably when the opportunity presents itself. Remember the saying, "give them a finger and they will take a hand?" When the Self-Aware Barbie shows up knowing it all, doing it all, and giving it all, it awakens entitlement and even predatory behavior in others. I personally seem to have a PhD in awakening the "I am entitled to your time and energy" response from all kinds of people. I have seen countless fully grown, capable people act like they own me. This has been a continued journey of inner work on my part.

You are a Self-Aware Barbie, if you…

- Are highly self-motivated and high achieving in your studies and career.

- Need to control everything and need things to be perfect to feel good.

- Feel like no one else can do it like you and often refuse support. What's the point when you will have to fix what they do anyways.

- Can juggle many tasks and to do lists, and are always looking to add more things to your plate.

- Have trouble relaxing and resting, there is always so much more to do.

- Often get taken advantage of in relationships because of your over giving and people pleasing nature.

- Typically outperform the men in your life in basically every area of life.

- Have trouble in romantic relationships because men are intimidated by you.

- Consider yourself and/or are considered by others an Alpha female.

- Look powerful on the outside but often feel weak and scared on the inside.

- Have trouble accessing your emotions and often feel numb to pleasure.

If this is you, you need feminine energy inner work yesterday!! Self-Aware Barbies make the ideal clients and students for my body of work. Through reclaiming your feminine power, nervous system reprogramming, and activating flow states, you become a healed whole being and start to function at full capacity. Imagine learning that one of your hands was tied behind your back all along. You accomplished all that you did with just one arm!! As amazing and admirable as that is, it's also exhausting. I have been there, and I know what that burn out feels like. Imagine what you could do and be if all of you were in sync and harmonious. This is what living in alignment truly means. You can find many resources, digital courses, and intensives to start your inner work journey on my website: www.theuniverseguru.com

The reason these two lower stages are becoming more and more common in society right now is because of the absence of maternal presence in the first 3 years of life. According to psychoanalyst, author, and parent coach Erica Komisar, there should be as little as possible separation between the mother and baby in the first 3 years.[17] Babies learn to manage their emotions and place in the world through attunement with their mother in these formative years. The mom not only needs to be physically but also emotionally present for the child to develop in a healthy way mentally and physically. Licensed professional counselor, Kelly McDaniel, refers to the absence of loving, safe, maternal presence in these early years as mother hunger, in her book, Mother Hunger.[18]

Modern day parents have been sold the lie of babies needing socialization in day cares and many who are able to stay home decide not to. The child, having been robbed with the attunement with the mother, develops coping mechanisms to deal with life. The Basic Babe becomes hungry for attention and affection and will resort to creating drama or problems to get attention from anyone, not realizing she internally deeply craves mother 's presence. This may start early on as a toddler throwing tantrums and a child in school unable to focus and learn. The Self-Aware Barbie chooses her achievements, over giving, over doing, people pleasing as her coping mechanism hoping to win the love that was her God given birth right all along.

This is not to blame mothers but allows parents to make the first 3 years the most important time for their children's entire life. Finding this research led to a double grieving process in my life. I first had to grieve the loss of not having my mother present and available when I was born, resulting in over 40 years of inner work. I know my mother wanted to be there, but my parents needed both incomes, and life was stressful for them as immigrants. Secondly, I had to grieve my first son's lack of maternal presence. When Armaan was born, I was in the middle of a very stressful divorce, a student at Northwestern University, and running a real estate business. He rarely had time with me. Contrary to popular belief, quality time is not the same as quantity of time. He needed me there all the time.

Luckily, both my son and I had the luxury of do-
ing inner work because we knew this as an option. It
makes me sad to think that most people spend their en-
tire life suffering and have no idea inner work was even
an option. I will now share with you the two healed
stages of consciousness from my work. Remembering
that healed doesn't mean your inner work has ended,
inner work happens in layers and there is always room
for improvement.

Million Dollar Babe

The Million Dollar Babe is the stage of feminine/mas-
culine healing and integration. In this stage, surrender
is a natural way of being because we trust in love and
feel safe in our body in the world. The Million Dollar
Babe lives in Divine flow, utilizing the beautiful struc-
tures she has created in her life. Because she is intuitive
and fully receptive to her spirit and angel guides, this
manifesting babe never feels or works alone. She is ful-
ly balanced and fluid in her masculine/feminine ener-
gies. This manifesting queen is vulnerable, sensual, and
fully embodied in her delicious worthiness. Her heart
is fully open and rests in warmth, faith, and love. This
is the "lucky bitch" stage where everyone assumes our
MDB is just born lucky, not realizing this is a learned
and embodied stage, and they too can activate it.

In this fully integrated frequency, the left and right
sides of the brain are perfectly in sync and working
together, giving you what may seem like superhuman
abilities. This means you are experiencing moments
of what is known as the zone or flow. Since you are

perfectly balanced in your feminine and masculine energies, you can switch and sway between the two very easily. This is how we would naturally be if the mother wound hadn't occurred in our early formative years. However, me and my clients and students have had to reparent ourselves to learn this essential way of living and being.

You are a Million Dollar Babe, if you...

- Are able to flow fluidly between your masculine and feminine energies.

- Know how and when to create polarity with your romantic partner.

- Trust that the world is good and the Universe is always working in your favor.

- Have no trouble manifesting your desires and normalizing them once they arrive.

- Are able to create money with ease and flow and exponentially grow your wealth through investing.

- Have a great relationship with your intuition and can make decisions easily.

- Live in your overflow and are able to feel and amplify pleasure in every area of your life.

- Are able to stay in your zone of genius and access flow states, making everything you touch turn to gold.

- Everyone around you thinks you were born lucky because you make everything look effortless and easy.

- Win in relationships because of your strong sense of self and energetic boundaries.

- Don't get triggered very often and know exactly how to process your emotions if you do without having to throw them out on anyone else.

If you identify with this stage, appreciate and enjoy everything you have created while still learning and expanding into more. Healed and whole people like you are essential role models for society. You are contributing to the morphogenetic field for all others around you. You may have your moments of doubt when you surround yourself with people who are suffering, but never feel guilty for what you have and who you are. Your unapologetic light and radiance are a necessary ingredient for the healing of all women on this planet, especially at this time. You are the 4-minute mile society needs right now, always remember that.

I offer many courses and intensives for women in the MBD stage who want to stand more confidently in their power. You can find these resources on my website.

High End Divinity

This is the stage of oneness in all things. In this stage, we move from manifesting it to becoming it. High End Divinity is my word for high priestess. In this stage you are more activated in your consciousness and metaphysical self than in your human animal self. In simple terms you are able to turn off the amygdala and keep that fight or flight response almost always turned off, increasing your presence in the now. This doesn't mean you spiritually bypass your human experience, but it does mean you are more aware of and connected with the spiritual aspects of your being. You are the observer versus the reactor to most things in life. Which eliminates very high or low emotional waves.

You are a High-End Divinity, if you…

- Have manifested everything you have desired and more for yourself, and now want to help others through your overflow.

- Rarely ever get triggered and actually end up helping the people triggering you.

- Give more than you take from the world and the quantum field.

- Are aware of other timelines and lifetimes beyond just this one.

- Are able to jump and collapse timelines at the speed of light.

If you identify with this stage, you have the ability to self regulate and coach yourself back into alignment and are probably only using me as a peer group grid to collaborate and create with.

My courses and coaching practice have now evolved to help women heal and create a ripple effect of healing on the planet. Just know that regardless of where you started and where you are right now, you always have the option to create a completely new reality for yourself. It will take lots of inner work and a complete overhaul of your identity, but it is possible.

When I married Irfan in 2008, I had so much inner work to do. Having the safety of his masculine providing and protection gave me the first safe place, time, and energy to start my healing journey. During the first edition of this book, I was further creating masculine structures in my life and activating more and more of my feminine energy. My wealthy woman era started as soon as I hit the Million Dollar Babe stage in 2016! I hope the process I shared with you in this book creates as much, if not more, success, healing, and love in your life as it has in mine.

We really can have it all if we dare to dream as much and remove all other options as possible realities. This book and my entire body of work represents not only one woman's journey but the collective awakening of women from all over the planet claiming their feminine power. I hope to have you as my next Million Dollar Babe testimonial.

Oceans of love,

Mina Irfan

August 24, 2023

REFERENCES

1. Lisle, Douglas J, and Alan Goldhamer. The Pleasure Trap. Summertown, Tenn.: Healthy Living Publications, 2003. Print.

2. Byrne, Rhonda, and Rhonda Byrne. The Secret. New York: Atria Books, 2006. Print.

3. The Secret. 2016. DVD.

4. D'Adamo, Peter, and Catherine Whitney. Eat Right 4 (For) Your Type. New York: G.P. Putnam's Sons, 1996. Print.

5. Davis, William. Wheat Belly. Emmaus, Penn.: Rodale, 2011. Print.

6. Davis, William. Wheat Belly Total Health. Print.

7. Greger, Michael, and Gene Stone. How Not To Die. Print.

8. Lipman, Frank. 10 Reasons You Feel Old And Get Fat. Print.

9. Durant, John, and Michael Malice. The Paleo Manifesto. Print.

10. Perlmutter, David, and Kristin Loberg. Brain Maker. Print.

11. Gottfried, Sara. The Hormone Reset Diet. Print.

12. Kondō, Marie, and Cathy Hirano. The Life-Changing Magic of Tidying Up. Print.

13. Tracy, Brian. *Eat That Frog!*. London: Hodder Mobius, 2004. Print.

14. Tierney, John. "Do You Suffer From Decision Fatigue?" *Nytimes.com*. N.p., 2011. Web. 3 Apr. 2016.

15. Stanley, Thomas J, and William D Danko. The Millionaire Next Door. Atlanta, Ga.: Longstreet Press, 1996. Print.

16. Stanley, Thomas J. *The Millionaire Mind*. Kansas City: Andrews McMeel Pub., 2000. Print.

17. Komisar, Erica. Being There: Why Prioritizing Motherhood in the First Three Years Matters. TarcherPerigee, 2017. Print.

18. McDaniel, Kelly. Mother Hunger. Hay House 2021. Print.

ADDITIONAL RESOURCES

Mina Irfan has over 60 digital courses available on her website at www.theuniverseguru.com in topics ranging from inner work, personal power, dating, relationships, parenting, health, and wealth.

She is also the Author of *Lady Balls: How to be Savagely Successful in a World Addicted to Suffering.*

ABOUT THE AUTHOR

Mina Irfan is a world renowned Author, Course Creator, Thought Leader, Life Coach, & Spiritual Mentor for High Performance, High Achieving Women looking to reconnect with their femininity. Her teachings are a combination of spiritual energy work plus her studies of Communications, Anthropology, and Evolutionary Psychology from Northwestern University. Thousands of women have been transformed through Mina's Personal Development, Inner Work, and SELF ACTUALIZATION content. Her digital courses have enrolled women from over a hundred countries representing CEO's, scientists, celebrities, famous influencers, doctors, to powerful stay at home moms and students looking to upgrade their quality of life through inner work. Mina Irfan stands for female empowerment through Inner work, Personal Responsibility, and Activating your Authentic Divine Feminine Power. She lives with her husband and 3 kids in Houston, Texas.

Acknowledgements

My deepest gratitude to my husband and children for their unlimited love and support throughout this book and all my projects. To my assistant, Henrietta Biró for her loving feedback, coaching, and professional editing.

And for you: without you asking for this book, it would have never been co-created.

Printed in Great Britain
by Amazon